PARENTS' RIGHTS

Books By John W. Whitehead

The Separation Illusion

Schools on Fire (with Jon T. Barton)

The New Tyranny

The Second American Revolution

The Stealing of America

Home Education and Constitutional Liberties (with Wendell R. Bird)

The Right to Picket and the Freedom of Public Discourse

Parents' Rights

The End of Man

The Rights of Religious Persons in Public Education

PARENTS' RIGHTS

John W. Whitehead

CROSSWAY BOOKS • WHEATON, ILLINOIS
A DIVISION OF GOOD NEWS PUBLISHERS

Parents' Rights.

Published by Crossway Books, a division of
Good News Publishers, 1300 Crescent Street, Wheaton, Illinois 60187

First printing, 1985

Printed in the United States of America

Library of Congress Catalog Card Number 85-70468

ISBN 0-89107-364-7

---

00 99 98 97 96 95 94 93 92
15 14 13 12 11 10 9 8 7 6 5

To R. J. Rushdoony

CONTENTS

PART V: PRACTICALITIES

ACKNOWLEDGMENTS

As with any book, there are those whose assistance moves the book along.

I appreciate Richard Moore's work on this book. His legwork and research were an important part of this project.

Kimberly Roberts' assistance and Dr. Daniel Osborne's advice were helpful. Thanks also goes to Lane and Jan Dennis for their encouragement and friendship.

The typing of the original manuscript was done by Pat Dwyer. She was very adept at meeting the deadlines.

Finally, I would like to thank my family. My wife, Carol, and five children—Jayson, Jonathan, Elisabeth, Joel, and Joshua—encouraged me in the process of writing this book. We all felt that this book was important enough to sacrifice to see that it became a reality.

John W. Whitehead

AUTHOR'S FOREWORD

George Orwell once wrote:

> The family could not actually be abolished, and, indeed, people were encouraged to be fond of their children in almost the old-fashioned way. The children, on the other hand, were systematically turned against their parents and taught to spy on them and report their deviation. The family had become in effect an extension of the Thought Police. It was a device by means of which everyone could be surrounded night and day by informers who knew him intimately.[1]

We have not quite progressed to the type of situation that Orwell describes. However, we must be cognizant of the fact that once the philosophical groundwork is laid, societies rapidly move into authoritarian modes.

Other elements necessary to what Orwell describes are present in modern Western societies. These are: fear, alienation, and loneliness.

We live in a lonely society. Modern people are alienated from one another. And the family—the one institution that constitutes the cultural glue that holds things together—is in trouble.

Moreover, parents today have the spirit of fear. Not only do they fear the threat of state intervention into family affairs, but they also distrust neighbors and friends who, on an increasing basis, report them for "suspected" child abuse.

In some ways this has become a national phobia. For example, Ronald Reagan in proclaiming April 1985 as "National Child Abuse Prevention Month" said:

> In the past decade, our knowledge of how to prevent and treat child abuse has grown substantially. The most important thing we have learned is that the active involvement of *neighbors and friends*—indeed of *everyone in a community*—is the key to success. Community child protection agencies cannot do the job alone but must rely on *neighbors, friends, teachers, doctors, and volunteers* to provide critical support, *information,* and guidance to families in which child maltreatment may occur.[2]

Although this proclamation is admirable in intent, it represents the concept of informers—or to some, the "Thought Police." It would be primarily informing on parents. And here the informers are "neighbors," "friends," and others.

Clearly, it is time that we discuss the hard issues confronting us—such as state intervention into the family, parents' rights, child abuse, and the like. Moreover, if we are to preserve traditional freedoms, we must also act to remedy the problems. However, it means doing more than talking about the issues or passing laws. Something much more fundamental than that is needed. It will mean touching and refurbishing the basic fabric of our culture.

I have written this book in hopes of making a positive comment on the problems facing parents, children, and families. Hopefully, we can do something to arrest the downward slide of our society. The future is ours. We only have to build it.

John W. Whitehead
Manassas, Virginia

PART ONE

THE ISSUES

[I]t is quite possible for a culture to exist without a social idea of children. Unlike infancy, childhood is a social artifact, not a biological category.

Professor Neil Postman
The Disappearance of Childhood (1982)

ONE

THE GREAT DIVORCE

The line between childhood and adulthood grows more blurred every year. In this book *The Disappearance of Childhood,* New York University professor Neil Postman argues convincingly that distinctions between children and adults are being eradicated.[1] There are growing evidences that this is occurring.

The children of today get a head start on puberty. They are sometimes a full three years ahead of earlier generations. This fact tends to lower the age of sexual experimentation—traditionally a landmark on the way to adulthood.

And children, at an early age, know more about the ways of the adult world today. Teachers in the classroom, television, and movies explore subjects that previous generations hardly knew existed—abortion, divorce, homosexuality, drug addiction, alcoholism.

Amid this onslaught, a corps of children's liberation advocates argue that children should in all respects be on an equal parity with adults. However, we must never forget that, no matter what happens, *children are still children.* This may seem obvious, but when it comes to the law and certain children's liberation advocates, the status of childhood becomes more confused.

Caught within this confusion, parents and their children are finding their relationships being challenged on an ever-increasing basis. If children are indeed to be treated as adults, then traditional parent-child relationships may be extirpated. This is evident in some recent cases.

THE DIVORCE

On June 18, 1973, Paul Snyder took his fifteen-year-old daughter Cynthia to the Youth Services Center of the Juvenile Department of King County Superior Court in Washington. For some time Cynthia had rebelled against her parents. As one court explained the situation:

> Cynthia's parents, being strict disciplinarians, placed numerous limitations on their daughter's activities, such as restricting her choice of friends, and refusing to let her smoke, date, or participate in certain extracurricular activities within the school, all of which caused Cynthia to rebel against their authority.[2]

Mr. and Mrs. Snyder hoped that the Juvenile Court Commissioner would "resolve the family dispute by admonishing Cyndy regarding her responsibilities to her parents."[3] Cynthia was placed in a receiving home.

A month later, however, Cynthia, with the help of caseworkers of the Department of Social and Health Services, filed a petition in court alleging that she was a dependent child under state law. The law defined a dependent child as one under eighteen years of age:

> who has no parent, guardian or other responsible person; or who has no parent or guardian willing to exercise, or capable of exercising, proper parental control; or . . . whose home by reason of neglect, cruelty or depravity of his parents or either of them, or on the part of his guardian, or on the part of the person in whose custody or care he may be, or for any other reason, is an unfit place for such child.[4]

Next, Cynthia was placed in the temporary custody of the Department of Social and Health Services, and an attorney was appointed her by the court. On October 12, approximately five months after the Snyders contacted the Juvenile Department, the Superior Court found no parental unfitness. The court ordered Cynthia to be returned to her parents' custody.

Cynthia remained with her parents for approximately one month. After more confrontations at home, she went to Youth

Advocates, a group which assists troubled juveniles. From there she was directed to the Youth Services Center.

On November 21, 1973, a state employee of the Youth Services Center filed a petition in court which alleged that Cynthia was incorrigible as defined by the law. Under this provision, a dependent child is one under eighteen years of age:

> who is incorrigible; that is, who is beyond the control and power of his parents, guardian, or custodian by reason of the conduct or nature of said child. . . .[5]

Cynthia, as a result of this petition, was placed in a foster home. A hearing was held several days later in which the court held that Cynthia was incorrigible. The case was appealed to the Washington Supreme Court.

To put things in perspective, it must be emphasized that Cynthia had no police record and, thus, there was no evidence that she was incorrigible in the traditional meaning of the term.[6] She lived all her life with her natural parents in a typical middle-class family. In an early phase of the case, the parents had been found to be "fit" parents in the statutory sense. And the parents were trying to keep the child within the authority of the family unit.

The Washington Superior Court framed the issue as "whether there is substantial evidence to support a finding that the parent-child relationship has dissipated to the point where parental control is lost and, therefore, Cynthia is incorrigible."[7] Then, finding "a total collapse" in the parent-child relationship, the court ruled the girl incorrigible.[8]

The *Snyder* case implies that a dissatisfied child should be permitted, as any adult would, to leave the family at her own request. Evidently it was Cynthia Snyder's decision that she preferred not to be subject to the authority of her parents. Her choice was upheld in the courts. The *Snyder* case is, therefore, an argument for the proposition that a child can "divorce," or at least achieve separation from, his or her parents on grounds of incompatibility.

But there is a more basic *divorce* involved here. As the dictionary defines "divorce," it means "to terminate" or separate "an existing relationship or union."[9] That is exactly what is happening in the American family. With the emergence of the "*adultified*" child (that is, a child who is treated as an adult), relationships within the family are being redefined. And a separation is occurring. In some instances family relationships are terminated. As a consequence, the children, as we have traditionally known them, are disappearing.

THREE STREAMS

As the *Snyder* case illustrates, there are three streams of influence affecting the traditional family structure.

The *first* is the rights of parents. Traditionally very strong, the rights of parents in contemporary society are being challenged.

Second, the concept of children's liberation is affecting the modern family. This movement goes beyond urging the rights of children. It, instead, argues that children are to be treated as if they are adults.

The *third* major force is actual or threatened intervention of the state into the family structure. Statist intervention grows more pervasive each day. This, combined with an indiscriminate and aggressive assertion of children's liberation, is a menace to legitimate family structures and the lawful exercise of parental rights.

For example, in the *Snyder* case the focus of the court (that is, the state) was on the best interest of the child, not the best interest of the family structure or the parents. The court said, "Our paramount consideration, irrespective of the natural emotions in cases of this nature, must be the welfare of the child."[10] Therefore, the state becomes an advocate on behalf of the child *against* the parents.

As will become evident, *there has occurred a continual shift toward the interest of children* in family situations where the state becomes involved. This is a clear break with history. If it continues to grow, many legitimate parental actions and practices will be brought into question on a perpetual basis.

TWO

THE ADULTIFIED CHILD

We must feel compassion for children in contemporary society. If they are not fortunate enough to be born into a stable family relationship, children receive little guidance from a culture steeped in relativistic values.

We must also feel concern for parents who strive to provide an adequate family structure, but who are caught in a continual clash with their children. As children are exposed to our modern antifamily culture, they are affected.

There is also a very dark side to the progressive move away from the family today. While our society has adultified children, it has also not allowed many adults to grow up. Immaturity and irresponsibility, therefore, mark our culture.

These facts, in conjunction with the basic "antilife" nature of Western society, have combined to form a devastating assault on *all* traditional structures. This means the past is painted as antiquated. But it also means that the future is up for grabs. All is uncertainty. And both parents and children are paying the price.

ABUSE

One basic way to judge the worth of any society is *the concern one generation has for the next generation.* If children and youth of a nation are protected and afforded the opportunity to develop their capacities to the fullest, then the prospects for the future are bright. "In contrast," Cornell University professor Urie Bronfenbrenner writes, "a society which neglects its children, however well it may function in other respects, risks eventual disorganization and demise."[1]

It is within the family that children have traditionally been cared for. However, the American family, especially outside the realm of those who hold traditional moral values, is in distress.

The breakdown of the family it taking on many aspects. "If we define the nuclear family as a working husband, a housekeeping wife, and two children, and ask how many Americans actually still live in this type of family," writes Alvin Toffler, "the answer is astonishing: 7 percent of the total United States population. Ninety-three percent of the population do not fit this ideal . . . model any longer."[2]

As the traditional family model has waned, the vacuum has been filled with what Toffler calls "a bewildering array of family forms."[3] "Homosexual marriages, communes, groups of elderly people banding together to share expenses (and sometimes sex), tribal groupings among certain ethnic minorities, and many other forms coexist as never before."[4]

Caught within this confusing matrix are children. Moreover, the devaluation of human life and erratic family patterns has continued to produce a violent onslaught against many children.

One study concerning child abuse conducted over a one-year period reveals some startling facts.[5] It was based on news reports of child abuse. There were 662 cases in all, involving some 557 families.

Of the cases reported, only 10 percent of the children were over age ten, and a preponderance fell below age four. Of 178 children who died as a result of abuse, over 80 percent were under age four and 53.98 percent were under age two. The parents were shown to be responsible for about 72.5 percent of the cases and 75.85 percent of the fatalities, with fathers being responsible for more total injuries, but mothers being responsible for a higher number of the fatalities. The following is a description from the report of some of the abuse:

> TYPES OF ABUSE
>
> The forms or types of abuse inflicted on these children is a negative testimony to the ingenuity and inventiveness of man. By far the greater number of injuries resulted from

beatings with various kinds of implements and instruments. The hairbrush was a common implement used to beat children. However, the same purpose was accomplished with deadlier impact by the use of bare fists, straps, electric cords, T.V. aerials, ropes, rubber hose, fan belts, sticks, wooden spoons, pool cues, bottles, broom handles, baseball bats, chair legs, and, in one case, a sculling oar. Less imaginative, but effective, was plain kicking with street shoes or with heavy work shoes.

Children had their extremities—hands, arms and feet—burned in open flames as from gas burners or cigarette lighters. Others bore burn wounds inflicted on their bodies with lighted cigarettes, electric irons or hot pokers. Still others were scalded by hot liquids thrown over them or from being dipped into containers of hot liquids.

Some children were strangled or suffocated by pillows held over their mouths or plastic bags thrown over their heads. A number were drowned in bathtubs and one child was buried alive.

To complete the list—children were stabbed, bitten, shot, subjected to electric shock, were thrown violently to the floor or against a wall, were stamped on and one child had pepper forced down his throat.

TYPES OF INJURIES

What kinds of injuries were inflicted on them?

The majority had various shapes, sizes and forms of bruises and contusions. There was a collection of welts, swollen limbs, split lips, black eyes and lost teeth. One child lost an eye.

Broken bones were common. Some were simple fractures; others compound. There were many broken arms, broken legs and fractured ribs. Many children had more than one fracture. One five month old child was found to have 30 broken bones in his little body.

The grimmest recital of all is the listing of internal injuries and of head injuries. The head injuries particularly were a sizeable group. Both the internal injuries and the head injuries were responsible for a great many of the fatalities. In this group we find damage to internal organs such as ruptured livers, ruptured spleens and ruptured lungs. Injuries to the head were concussions or skull frac-

> tures, with brain hemorrhage and brain damage a frequent diagnosis.
>
> This is indeed a grim, sad, sordid and horror-filled recital of what happens to children in communities in almost every State of the Union. It is made all the more so by the fact that this represents a compilation of specific situations—a cumulative report of the findings in 662 different cases.[6]

Another study indicates that the abused or battered child is not peculiar to any single economic or social group.[7] The problem is found in the poorer slum areas and the "country club districts" and arises from both culturally deprived families and families in higher business and professional groupings.[8]

A 1984 report by the United States Department of Justice on *Family Violence* confirms the problem of child abuse. It noted:

> Ascertainable reported cases of child abuse and neglect have doubled from 1976 to 1981. In addition to the one million reported cases of child maltreatment, there may be yet another million unreported cases. Untold numbers of children are victims of sexual abuse and uncounted older persons suffer abuse.[9]

Again, as the Justice Department report found, "family violence cuts across all racial and economic lines. Victims of physical and sexual abuse come from all types of homes, even the very 'best' of families."[10]

There are many specific examples of child abuse. Let me cite a few actual cases.

One concerned the death of a two-year-old girl named Jennifer. According to her mother's testimony, Jennifer had apparently died of a severe blow on the head. Her father allegedly dismembered her body and left it for rubbish collection in a plastic trash bag. At the time of her death, her parents were under investigation for the abuse of their four-year-old son as well.

Not long after this case, the body of a five-month-old girl was also found in a plastic bag awaiting rubbish collection. Her parents claimed that she had suffocated.

Another case involved an eleven-year-old girl named Diane.

She died of a blood clot on the brain which was apparently caused by blows to the head. Diane was reportedly beaten daily for two weeks and continuously for eight hours before she died.

Obviously, then, there is a legitimate argument that says children should have the *right* to be free from such abuse. The question concerns how and when that right should be exercised and to what degree the state should enforce such a right.

CHILDREN'S LIBERATION

The stark reality of child abuse is that *it is parents who abuse children.* And it is parents from all walks of life.

However, many parents do not abuse children. They also believe that child abuse is morally wrong. These are good parents who believe that their children are precious and, correspondingly, protect them.

It is this type of parent that appropriately has the right to *a* form of sovereign control over his children. This control, of course, is limited only to the traditional exceptions recognized in civilized societies. However, the children's liberation movement threatens to eradicate all parental control over children.

There are two conceptions of childhood that are huddled under the banner of the "children's rights movement." They appear to be opposed to each other, but in many respects are parallel movements.

One of them believes that childhood is desirable although fragile. The advocates of this view argue for protection of children from neglect and abuse. Such advocates would argue for intervention of the state when parental responsibility fails.

The other conception of "child's rights" is that of liberation. It rejects adult supervision and control of children. It also provides a philosophy to justify the dissolution of childhood. Advocates of this philosophy, as Neil Postman points out, argue "that the social category 'children' is in itself an oppressive idea and that everything must be done to free the young from its restrictions."[11] But this concept is not new. As Postman notes, this view has its origins "in the Dark and Middle Ages *when there were no 'children'* in the modern sense of the word."[12]

The outer limits are represented by such people as Richard

Farson who argues for complete rights for children. Farson advocates the following list of rights for children:

1. *The Right to Self-Determination:* Children should have the right to decide matters that affect them most directly.
2. *The Right to Alternate Home Environments:* Self-determining children should be able to choose from among a variety of arrangements; residences operated by children, child-exchange programs, twenty-four hour child-care centers, and various kinds of schools and employment opportunities.
3. *The Right to Responsive Design:* Society must accommodate itself to children's size and to their need for safe space.
4. *The Right to Information:* A child must have the right to all information ordinarily available to adults—including, and perhaps especially, information that makes adults uncomfortable.
5. *The Right to Educate Oneself:* Children should be free to design their own education, choosing from among many options the kinds of learning experiences they want, including the option not to attend any kind of school.
6. *The Right to Freedom from Physical Punishment:* Children should live free of physical threat from those who are larger and more powerful than they.
7. *The Right to Sexual Freedom:* Children should have the right to conduct their sexual lives with no more restriction than adults.
8. *The Right to Economic Power:* Children should have the right to work, to acquire and manage money, to receive equal pay for equal work, to choose trade apprenticeship as an alternative to school, to gain promotion to leadership positions, to own property, to develop a credit record, to enter into binding contracts, to engage in enterprise, to obtain guaranteed support apart from the family, to achieve financial independence.
9. *The Right to Political Power:* Children must possess the same political rights as adults, such as voting, holding office and the like.

10. *The Right to Justice:* Children must have the guarantee of a fair trial with due process of law, an advocate to protect their rights against parents as well as the system, and a uniform standard of detention.[13]

Farson would adultify children. Parental protections would be eliminated. Inevitably, however, this would mean parent/adult-child conflicts. This would necessitate state intervention. In other words, as private restraints on childhood are lessened, statist restraints on both adults and children increase.

Farson's ideas are not merely isolated academic arguments. They are representative of a large cross-section of people. Some of these people are in the position of placing the force of law behind their ideology. One such person is Patricia Wald, who sits as a federal judge on the United States Court of Appeals for the District of Columbia. This is one of the most powerful courts in America.

Comparing the "institution of children" to the "institution of slavery," Wald advocates that children need legal representation independent of their parents.[14] In a 1976 article in the *Journal of the Child Welfare League of America* she wrote: "In situations where the interests of the child and parents are likely to conflict and a serious adverse impact on the child is likely to be the consequence of unilateral parental actions, the child's interests deserve representation by an independent advocate before a neutral decision maker. . . . A child should have access to free or paid legal services on a confidential basis to discuss his personal grievances."[15]

Rejecting the traditional family design, Wald argues for the "equality of all family members."[16] Concerning school and work, Wald advocates: "From the age of seven on, a youth should be able to exercise increasing control over his choice of school and work or, at the very least, to participate fully in making decisions affecting this vital area of life."[17]

On medical care, Wald states that "[c]ertainly from 12 on, a youth ought to be able to seek medical or psychiatric care of his own."[18] Concerning parental notification of such care, Patricia Wald notes: "In some instances (contraception, abortion, drugs, VD, psychiatric help) disclosure may spell disastrous consequences for this child within his family and thus deter him from ever]seeking help. Incest, a psychotic parent, or even a *frantically moralistic one,* are cases in point."[19]

To eliminate confusion between parental rights and children's rights concerning medical care, Wald proposes a form of legislation "vesting right to engage in such services in youth, rather than in their parents."[20] In claiming the need for an "emancipation proclamation . . . for teenage children,"[21] Wald states that "youth ought presumptively to enjoy a whole range of civil rights."[22]

HYSTERIA

Amid the drive by children's rights advocates to stamp out child abuse, "the fantasies of youngsters," writes Ted Gest in *U.S. News and World Report,* "are causing nightmares for innocent adults."[23] He adds that "many observers say the flurry of arrests and new laws aimed at easing the trauma of young victims sometimes misfires, creating a child-abuse hysteria."[24]

Recent cases seem to support the notion of hysteria. However, it is not just parents; *other adults* are also affected. Gest notes:

> Brian Taugher, a top aide to California's attorney general, was acquitted of molesting a 4-year-old girl, but not before his reputation was ruined and his bank account emptied by legal fees.
>
> Authorities dropped charges against all but one of 25 persons accused during a massive sex-abuse probe in the tiny town of Jordon, Minn.
>
> Hermenia Albo, a 60-year-old grandmother, was charged with abusing students at a New York City day-care center. After a grand jury refused to indict her, she sued for false arrest.[25]

This means, as journalist Al Haas notes in *The Philadelphia Inquirer,* "the creation of a new kind of victim":

> The increased reporting brings with it an increase in the number of false or unfounded reports. This means that

> more people are being unjustly accused of child sexual abuse, that more people are being subjected to hellish, often expensive ordeals.
>
> People across the country who have been unjustly accused now are banding together to protect themselves and others through a new organization called Victims of Child Abuse Laws (VOCAL).[26]

VOCAL contends that "governmental child-protection agencies frequently savage families through high-handed, insensitive investigations that . . . 'assume you are guilty until proven innocent.' "[27] This creates fear.

> The threat of such unfounded accusations has also left the people and institutions that work with children deeply fearful. Increasingly, teachers and staff members at elementary schools, day-care centers and summer day camps are worrying that they might be on the receiving end of a career-destroying allegation.
>
> Suddenly, these adults in the business of helping children are wondering whether hugging a child, taking him to the bathroom or counseling him in private will lead to an abuse charge—and a ruined reputation and vocation.[28]

Clearly, parents (and other adults), children, and the state are on a collision course if present trends continue. This is especially so in light of the emphasis on "emotional abuse or deprivation" as being part of the definition of child abuse.

Childhelp USA, a national organization designed to prevent child abuse, in a pamphlet emphasizes that "[c]hild abuse consists of any act of commission or omission that endangers or impairs a child's physical or emotional health and development."[29] The pamphlet explains:

> The negative effects of emotional abuse can be as devastating to a child's development emotionally, intellectually, and behaviorally as are injuries sustained by physical abuse. . . . Although this type of abuse is often difficult to recognize and identify, *the best interests of the child* should be the first concern in reporting this type of abuse. Close attention should be given when it is suspected that the emotion-

> al abuse is the result of a willful act creating mental suffering for the child.
>
> Since emotional abuse often has no visible physical signs, there are those who have resorted to inflicting this type of abuse on *their* child believing it is less likely to be reported. Therefore, awareness of the potential harm of this type of abuse is crucial.[30]

Anyone with an average imagination could conjure up various kinds and types of mental and emotional stress. They easily range from teaching the Bible to children to restricting the sexual activities of young teens.

Underlying the emotional/mental stress arguments are two presuppositions. These are brought out forcefully in the Childhelp USA pamphlet. First, a "child abuser is usually a person closely related to the child such as a parent, step-parent, or other caretaker."[31] Second, not only do the abused need help, but also "[a]busers need help."[32]

These parent or "caretaker" abusers need to be reported. This is "the first step in [the] . . . helping process."[33] In other words, it is suggested that one is doing parents a "favor" to turn them in to the authorities.

In this respect, Childhelp USA provides a toll-free telephone number to call in order to report parents and others "upon suspicion" that they may be child abusers.[34] Eventually, the state is called into these situations.

CHILD ABUSE LAWS

This mentality is facilitated by the fact that the law supports and undergirds it. For example, many child abuse laws speak of "mental or emotional" impairment as part of child abuse.

In New York, the statutory definition of a "neglected child" is, among other things, one whose "mental or emotional condition has been impaired or is in imminent danger of becoming impaired as a result of the failure of his parent to exercise a minimum degree of care."[35] The statute then goes on to provide a nonexclusive definition for "impairment of emotional health" and "impairment of mental or emotional condition":

> These terms include, but are not limited to, a state of substantially diminished psychological or intellecutal functioning in relation to, but not limited to, such factors as failure to thrive, control of aggressive or self-destructive impulses, ability to think and reason, or acting out or misbehavior, including incorrigibility, ungovernability, or habitual truancy; provided however, that such impairment must be clearly attributable to the unwillingness or inability of the respondent to exercise a minimum degree of care toward the child.[36]

New York's inclusion of the child's mental and emotional condition as being protected under the child abuse and neglect laws is consistent with the broadly worded "purpose clause" of the enactment. It states:

> This article is designed to establish procedures to help protect children from injury or mistreatment and to help safeguard their physical, mental, and emotional well-being. It is designed to provide a due process of law for determining when the state, *through its family court, may intervene against the wishes of a parent on behalf of a child so that his needs are properly met.*[37]

Other states have child abuse and neglect provisions which are similarly broad and inclusive, giving the courts wide discretion concerning what constitutes a violation of these acts. For example, in Connecticut abuse includes the vague term "emotional maltreatment," and a child may be found "neglected" who "is being denied proper care and attention, physically, educationally, emotionally or morally" or "is being permitted to live under conditions, circumstances or associations injurious to his well-being."[38]

In Montana, an "abused or neglected child" means "a child whose normal physical or mental health or welfare is harmed or threatened with harm by the acts or omissions of his parent." "Harm" means "the harm that occurs whenever the parent or other person responsible for the child's welfare inflicts or allows to be inflicted upon the child physical or mental injuries, including injuries sustained as a result of excessive corporal punishment." And "mental injury" means "an identifiable and substantial impairment of the child's intellectual and psychological functioning."[39]

In Arizona, prior to a recent revision, the definition of "abuse" was extremely broad:

> "Abuse" means the infliction of physical or mental injury or the causing of deterioration of a child and shall include failing to maintain reasonable care and treatment or exploiting or overworking a child to such an extent that his health, morals or emotional well-being is endangered.[40]

This language was later constricted to include only "the infliction of severe emotional damage" as evidenced by specific symptoms (in addition to the infliction of physical injuries).[41]

Similarly, in 1962 the Idaho legislature authorized intervention for "neglect" where a child was "emotionally maladjusted" or where a child who had been denied proper parental love or affectionate association "behaves unnaturally and unrealistically in relation to normal situations, objects, and other persons."[42]

EXPLOITATION

Parents, therefore, have a reason to be concerned. Parental authority is seemingly being undermined.

Moreover, if the advocates of the radical children's liberation movement have their way, children will be placed in the cold world of adults. They will be adultified.

We must never forget, however, that *children are not miniature adults*. They are entirely distinct from adults physically and psychologically. That is why parental authority has been exerted over them in the past.

Adultifying children removes this protection, the loss of which has been played out in modern society with devastating results. The alarming rise of children used as sex objects in the rapidly growing children's pornography business should be enough to raise cries for more protection of children.

Sexual abuse and exploitation of children has reached major

proportions in many areas of American society. As Lloyd Shearer could write in June 1985:

> Last year, seven teachers in a California day-care center were accused of 208 counts of molestation involving more than 100 children. In a small Minnesota town, it was alleged that parents swapped and sexually abused their offspring. In Washington, D.C., Sen. Paula Hawkins (R., Fla.) revealed she had been sexually molested as a child.
>
> Pedophilia, the adult lust for children, is no longer an esoteric medical word. Social scientists and politicians have taken up the fight against it. The government is hard at work issuing child-safety handbooks to parents; providing guidance on the prevention of sexual abuse in homes, day-care centers and schools; and overseeing the Head Start program, which serves some 450,000 preschoolers from low-income families and employs about 75,000 workers.
>
> Several weeks ago, Margaret Heckler, the Secretary of Health and Human Services, released a report on child neglect and abuse in which she revealed the following shockers:
>
> • One in every four or five girls and one in every nine or 10 boys, it is estimated, are sexually abused before they reach 18.
>
> • In almost 98% of known cases, the child is abused in the home by close relatives, family friends or neighbors. The single largest group of abusers (77%) are parents.
>
> • Sexual abusers come from all socioeconomic backgrounds, and as many as 75% were sexually abused as children. . . .
>
> • Some abusers threaten children into compliance. Others cleverly persuade them to accept guilt for their own victimization.[43]

The actual use of children for sexual purposes is, therefore, rampant.

Our society is effectively removing the protections traditionally afforded children. The family, the one institution that has traditionally afforded the most protection for children, is being systematically undermined.

We are now witnessing an entire generation of "unfamilied" people, with little or no concept of what it means to be a parent, attempting to have families. Parents and children alike are suffering. And unfortunately, American society is doing little to cure the problem, except to corrode the one institution—the family—that can remedy the situation. Thus, more and more children will continue to stand unprotected against an adult world that exploits them.

THREE

THE MEDIATING STRUCTURE

In a 1982 editorial, the *San Francisco Examiner* observed that the "notion that an unmarried relationship is the equivalent of marriage is an attack upon social norms, the destruction of which concerns a great many people in the nation and, we assume, in San Francisco."[1] Shortly thereafter, San Francisco's Board of Supervisors approved an unprecedented ordinance authorizing the payment of spousal benefits to unmarried partners who share "the common necessaries of life" with city employees.[2]

At the Baltimore session of the 1980 White House Conference on the Family, one delegate asked the conference to define the family as "two or more persons who share resources, responsibility for decisions, values and goals, and have commitment to one another over time." This proposal lost by only two votes among 761 delegates.[3]

Clearly, there is much discussion on American family life. However, as these incidents suggest, Americans "are having increasing difficulty even agreeing about what a 'family' is."[4] One law professor, for example, has argued that there should be a constitutional right that would give any "intimate association" between two persons the same protection as the law now gives to traditional relationships based on marriage.[5]

Those who sit on the courts, as well as others, have a blurred view of the family and what traditionally were family functions. For instance, the New York Court of Appeals in 1980 extended the "constitutional right of privacy" to protect the right of unmarried adults to seek "sexual gratification."[6]

While sexual privacy may at first seem unrelated to the issue of family forms, this case was a key factor in the subsequent decision of a lower New York court in 1981 to allow one adult male to adopt another adult male.[7] On a variation of the privacy theory, the Pennsylvania Supreme Court has given constitutional protection to sex acts performed in a public lounge between dancing performers and lounge patrons.[8]

Thus, the idea of sexual privacy outside traditional marriage has, in most respects, become a part of the basic law. The older concept that such practices were to be protected only within the family unit has been eradicated.

With the decline in the sacrosanctness of the family, however, at least two effects are evident. First, the needs of children are neglected, and as a result children are harmed. Second, the power of the state is increased. If these effects are not stalled, they will have a devastating impact on the stability of American society.

THE NEEDS OF CHILDREN

In their "Bill of Rights for Children," Henry Foster and Doris Freed argue that a "child has a moral right and should have a legal right . . . [t]o receive parental love and affection, discipline and guidance, and to grow to maturity in a home environment which enables him to develop into a mature and responsible adult."[9]

This concept, of course, is not new. It was, as professor Bruce Hafen notes, "at the very foundation of the juvenile court movement since the turn of the century."[10] Both Jeremy Bentham[11] and John Locke[12] urged similar concepts. In this way the young were to be prepared to enter society as mature and rational beings. However, this most basic of children's "rights"—the right to be prepared by parents for the responsibilities of adult life—has remained essentially *a moral, rather than a legal, duty of parents*. This is because the law is essentially "powerless to endorse such broad affirmative obligations."[13]

Despite what parents can be "forced" to do, the conditions that optimize "a home environment which enables [a child] to develop into a mature and responsible adult"[14] are clearly encouraged by cultural patterns that support family foundations. Moreover, legal protection of parental autonomy and family stability create a sense of permanency and stable expectations in child-parent relations.

It is evident that the needs of the child must be met in the family or they are likely not to be met.[15] Empirical studies establish beyond question that "the need of every child for unbroken continuity of affectionate and stimulating relationships, surroundings, and environmental influence are essential for a child's normal development."[16] This is family stability.

The child's need for family stability is so great, one author argues, that disruptions of the parent-child relationship *by the state*—even when there appears to be inadequate parental care—frequently do more harm than good.[17] In fact, research data from a variety of fields and sources confirm in "study after study" how "vital the family is in the crucial areas of individual motivation, personality structure, and creativeness."[18]

The bottom line is that traditional family structure, if it is supported and protected by its culture, works. This is seen by the "experiments" conducted in other countries concerning traditional family structure. The Soviet Union is one example.

Russia has retreated considerably from its earlier attempts to implement the Marxist demand that traditional family structure be altered because it perpetuated capitalistic property ideas. For Friedrich Engels and Karl Marx, marriage and legitimacy were counterproductive. Children were to be brought into collectives rather than parental homes. In 1926, the conclusion and termination of Russian marriage were purely private transactions.[19]

By 1944, however, new state regulation of marriage, divorce, and illegitimacy was introduced by the Soviet government. This was partly through considerations of population policy. But there was also another reason:

> The strengthening of the family . . . had become necessary because of the communist state's interest in the welfare of the nation's offspring as well as its fear that the national strength and vigor might be sapped by the laxity of morals, sexual and otherwise. The public institutions for child care had been developed vigorously. To a considerable extent

> they freed women for work outside the home, but they were far from totally replacing the home as classical Marxist theory had expected them rapidly to do.[20]

It is interesting that the very philosophy that the Soviets appear to be abandoning is being implemented in America. This is true even in light of the results of sociological and psychological studies which show that the opposite should be true.

These studies are beginning to raise doubts about the value of dominant state intervention in family concerns. As we are beginning to see, such a state-backed philosophy has numerous effects.

One such effect is evident in terms of parents themselves. Children's liberation advocates not only ignore the real needs of children. They also create with adults the false expectation that they, too, can be—or should be—*liberated* "from the arduous demands of a parental and community commitment to child-rearing."[21] The resultant consequence is, again, family *in*stability.

It is evident that the best place for children to grow up is a healthy family structure. This means that parents must be present with (not liberated from) and have intimate contact with their children. As Christopher Lasch writes:

> [T]he best argument for the indispensability of the family [is] that children grow up best under . . . conditions of "intense emotional involvement" [with their parents]. . . . Without struggling with the ambivalent emotions aroused by the union of love and discipline in his parents, the child never masters his inner rage or has fear of authority. *It is for this reason that children need parents, not professional nurses and counselors.*[22]

Studies now indicate that children who psychologically adjusted in a traditional structure cope with the concept of authority much better than those who have experienced unstable conditions. Such a child learns to deal with the so-called "father figure" in ways that enable him to succeed his father rather than eliminate him. In other words, the child productively comes to terms with the whole concept of authority.[23]

As a consequence, Lasch notes, the child is able "to internalize moral standards in the form of a conscience."[24] Without such an experience, *the child never grows up*. "Psychologically he remains in important ways a child," Lasch writes, "surrounded by authorities with whom he does not identify and whose authority he does not regard as legitimate."[25]

The "child who-never-grows-up" syndrome is evident in modern American society—which is basically a culture of irresponsibility. This is, in large part, a result of the breakdown in traditional family structures.

Of course, we cannot say that all traditional families are stable. Not all necessarily provide wholesome continuity for their children—as the prevailing levels of child abuse and divorce amply illustrate. However, the *commitments* inherent in formal families do increase the likelihood of stability and continuity for children. As professor Hafen notes:

> Those factors are as essential to child development that they alone may justify the legal incentives and preferences traditionally given to permanent kinship units based on marriage. The same factors can justify the denial of legal protection of unstable social patterns that threaten children's developmental environment.[26]

MEDIATING STRUCTURES

Modern society has, in many ways, taken over basic family functions. One such function is *socialization*—that is, preparing the child to enter society. This is done primarily through the public education system.

As a consequence, the state has become more involved and has, through its agencies (including the courts), subjected family socialization to increasingly effective control. Thus, having weakened the capacity for self-direction and self-control, American society, along with the state, "has undermined one of the principal sources of social cohesion, only to create new ones more constricting than the old, and ultimately more devastating in their impact on personal and political freedom."[27]

With the increasing loss of the traditional family structure, society is being deprived of its basic "mediating structure." Mediating structures are such institutions as neighborhoods, families, churches, schools, and voluntary associations. When intact, they limit the growth of the state. As Peter Berger and Richard John Neuhaus write:

> Without institutionally reliable processes of mediations, the political order becomes detached from the values and realities of individual life. Deprived of its moral foundation, the political order is "delegitimated." When that happens, the political order must be secured by coercion rather than by consent. And when that happens, democracy disappears.
>
> The attractiveness of totalitarianism . . . is that it overcomes the dichotomy of private and public existence by imposing on life one comprehensive order of meaning.[28]

Mediating structures—especially the family—are "the value-generating and value-maintaining agencies in society."[29]

Therefore, when these structures break down, society—that is, people—must look to the megastructures, such as the state, as a source of values. In America, we see the state-financed public schools assuming the role of providing "values." The totalitarian state gladly and aggressively assumes this role. *It becomes a substitute family.*

Berger and Neuhaus assert that the concept of mediating structures identifies the family as "the major institution within the private sphere, and thus for many people the most valuable thing in their lives. Here they make their moral commitments, invest their emotions, [and] plan for the future."[30] The family's traditional role in providing emotional and spiritual comfort, as well as human fulfillment, "has long been a dominant theme in sociological literature."[31]

There is, however, an even more political meaning to the traditional family's place as a mediating structure in American society. If families are allowed to operate unfettered, they produce the form of diversity and pluralism that is essential to free societies. This avoids the uniformity that is associated with authoritarian states.

Again, however, the key in free societies is maintaining a family structure that teaches fundamental values to children. As professors Philip Heymann and Douglas Barzelay comment:

> In democractic theory as well as the practice, it is in the family that children are expected to learn the values and beliefs that democratic institutions later draw on to determine group directions. The immensely important power of deciding about matters of early socialization has been allocated to the family, not to the government.[32]

SOCIAL PARENTING

Our culture is facing both the liberation of children and parents simultaneously. To resolve this crisis, *institutionalization* of children has come to the forefront as the obvious answer to the problem of "what to do with the children." Moreover, as these movements continue to progress, there will be a stronger, albeit subtle, push for more state-financed day-care centers (and even starting children in the public or state-approved private schools at a younger age).

For the first 185 years of its existence, the United States was characterized by a cultural system that considered child-rearing the responsibility of each family. Children, it was assumed, were properly raised in the home. State intervention was justified only in cases of family malfunction. Nonmaternal child care, in particular, was considered to be a mark of abnormality.

During the 1920s, however, a new ideology of "social parenting" began to take shape in America. It was argued that under modern industrial conditions the family was losing its function, and experts were needed to fill the vacuum.

> Gender-free, noncompetitive playthings properly presented in a day-care center . . . could produce a new generation of children, trained to be *independent in their moral judgments* yet cooperative in their social activities.[33]

Seen in this way, the view of nursery or day care was transformed in some professional circles from a limited service for families in trouble into a desirable stage in every child's life. From there, such people as anthropologist Margaret Mead could suggest that full-time mothering actually was somewhat abnormal. The answer to this abnormal situation was state-financed day-care centers.[34] As a takeoff from Mead, one social worker concluded that "day care can offer something valuable to children *because they are separated from their parents*."[35]

Eventually, state-financed child-care facilities were seen as necessary. At the National Organization for Women's 1970 Annual Conference, NOW declared that "[c]hild care must become a political priority."[36] There was, thus, a call "to exert pressure on the power structure in labor, industry and government to immediately make available facilities, funds, etc. and to grant tax deductions for quality child care."[37]

The report of the 1970 White House Conference on Children likewise advocated social parenting. Decrying existing federal legislation resting on a "narrow and static" concept of the family and celebrating "our pluralistic culture of varying family forms and a multiplicity of cultures," the conference found the "traditional model of the biological mother as the sole and constant caretaker" to be "unusual." It cited "new" research demonstrating day care to be "highly beneficial to the social and intellectual functioning of children."[38]

As the day-care concept has caught on, one thing is clear. Historian Bernard Greenblatt writes: "For the first time in the nation's history, social parentage competes effectively with families on a mass basis for influence over the preschool-age child."[39]

Less clear is the effect of cradle-to-adolescence institutionalization on children. One writer states:

> There is . . . substantial research suggesting that the depersonalization inherent in the group care of children under the age of three commonly causes "anaclitic depression" and other psychological disorders. Strong evidence exists suggesting that universal day care in the Soviet Union—in place for many decades now—has resulted in an epidemic of psychological disorders.[40]

In Sweden, where several decades of pressures and incentives have substantially eliminated the full-time mother, results are also not encouraging. State-financed public day care in Sweden has recently been criticized as "a loveless storage place":

> The failure of day care to create the promised "new" individual has also led to calls for more coercion aimed at "breaking down the isolation of families as units" and forcing men to act more like mothers. As a probable consequence, ever fewer young Swedes are bothering to marry or bear children.[41]

Despite the questionable nature of mass state-financed day care, it is still being heavily promoted in this country. For example, a 1982 interview in *Working Women* magazine of nine top corporate women reveal their belief that the basic method of breaking male dominance in the business world is having more women in the work force. This raised the question of what to do with children of working mothers. The answer was state-financed day-care centers.[42]

Monolithic control of the value transmission system is "a hallmark of totalitarianism."[43] For obvious reasons, then, the state nurseries or day-care centers are the paradigm for a totalitarian society. Clearly, *an "essential element in maintaining a system of limited government is to deny state control over child-rearing.*"[44] This is simply because child-rearing has such power. It determines the future mindset of the citizenry.

Even if the system of transmitting values were to remain less than monolithic, massive state involvement with child-rearing would invest the government "with the capacity of influencing powerfully . . . the future outcomes of . . . [the] political process."[45] And even, as is true in this country, if the people remained "free" to believe and speak as they wish, it would not diminish the immense impact of centralized value and beliefs transmission instilled in the people.[46]

Finally, the vitality of the traditional family form is not totally dependent on its key function of value transmission in child-rearing. In fact, marriage alone plays a critical role in the structure of free societies by interposing a significant legal entity between the individual and the state. As one writer has recognized:

> *[T]he marriage bond . . . is the fundamental connecting link in Christian society. Break it, and you will have to go back*

> *to the overwhelming dominance of the State, which existed before the Christian era.* The Roman State was all-powerful, the Roman Fathers represented the State, the Roman family was the father's estate, held more or less in fee for the State itself. It was the same in Greece, with not so much feeling for the permanence of property, but rather a dazzling splash or the moment's possessions. . . .
>
> But, in either case, the family was the man, as representing the State. There are States where the family is the woman: or there have been. There are States where the family hardly exists, priest States where the priestly control is everything, even functioning as family control. Then there is the Soviet State, where again family is not supposed to exist. . . .
>
> Now the question is, do we want to go back, or forward, to any of these forms of State Control? . . . [P]erhaps the greatest contribution to the social life of man made by Christianity is—marriage. . . . Christianity established the little autonomy of the family within the greater rule of the State. Christianity made marriage . . . not to be violated by the State. It is marriage, perhaps, which has given man the best of his freedom, given him his little kingdom of his own within the big kingdom of the State, given him his foothold of independence on which to stand and resist an unjust State. Man and wife, a king and queen with one or two subjects, and a few square yards of territory of their own: this, really, is marriage. *It is true freedom.*[47]

STANDING ON THE EDGE

Diversity and limited government are assured through a private property system that has traditionally been related to family control. Unfortunately, family control of property has been greatly diminished in recent years.

Moreover, the familiar family function of providing social services for the sick, the young, and the disabled "not only provides the psychological nurturing of personalized care, but also prevents the state from assuming economic leverage and political power that would accompany total state responsibility for welfare functions."[48]

With the onslaught against the family coming so strongly

from many directions, the family and its functions are being subsumed by the state. We are standing on the edge of a fundamental crisis. We are haunted by the spectre of Big Brother or, possibly, Big Sister.

We really have no choice but to strengthen the basic functions of the family. Here, and especially here, there are clear patterns in history and logic that can teach us much.

P A R T   T W O

THE FAMILY PATTERN

Families were meant to be a continuity with generation following generation—not a confused mixture of splinters as broken as the scattered families of refugees. How many real refugees there are in the world, made up of frustrated people trying to find out who they are, if you count all the broken relationships in thrice, or twice, or once divorced couples and their children! They cling to bits of wreckage seeking some solid ground to start life on the other side of the divorce—as stormy a body of water to cross as any gale-blown gulf or sea of ocean.

Edith Schaeffer
Lifelines (1982)

FOUR

INVENTING CHILDHOOD

The history of parent-child relationships in the ancient pagan world is one of domination by parents and adults. Infanticide, ritual exposure, mutilation, and abandonment of children were common to many ancient societies. These practices derived from a low view of life that was later remedied in part by the coming of Christianity. Unfortunately, these pagan practices are reemerging in contemporary societies.

INFANTICIDE

Infanticide—the killing of new*born* infants with explicit or implied consent of parents and community—was once a form of birth control, a way of avoiding the embarrassment of an illegitimate child, a way of disposing of a weak or deformed child, and a means of serving religious beliefs. Ironically, the ancient practice of infanticide, outlawed by the older civilized societies, has now reared its ugly head in contemporary society—mainly through the logical consequences of the abortion movement.

Various religions have required that the firstborn be sacrificed to appease a god or gods. In some societies, female children were sacrificed because they were either considered useless or inferior to male children. (Again, this practice has been revived in countries such as Communist China where female infanticide is being practiced on a wide scale.)[1] Abandonment or exposure to the elements of a child who was unwanted or who could not be provided for was a form of infanticide that was common in ancient societies.[2]

GREECE AND ROME

In Greece a child was the absolute property of his father, "who had to decide whether he would live or die."[3] On the fifth day after birth, at the ceremony of Amphidromia, the father was forced to decide whether or not to receive the infant into the family.

Under Greek law, property was divided among the *male* children. As professor Mason Thomas writes:

> Thus, the father might be inclined to raise the first son, while the second would be exposed in order not to dilute the inheritance. Girls were less important and more frequently exposed. The task of exposing a child was performed by a slave or midwife, who would take him to a public place early in the day, hoping that he might be rescued. Often, valuable objects were left with the child as an inducement to rescue.[4]

Under ancient Roman law the father had a power of life and death over his children that extended into adulthood. He could kill, mutilate, sell, or offer his child in sacrifice. During periods of prosperity a Roman father might sell the services of his son under an arrangement akin to an apprenticeship or a labor contract.[5]

Later, reforms were instituted to curtail some of these practices. No child was allowed to be killed before the age of three. Male children were to be saved. Later the law permitting infanticide was abolished (although infants could be sold into slavery). Under Emperor Hadrian, a father who had killed his grown son for committing a crime was banished from the empire.[6]

In Old Testament times numerous pagan religions practiced child sacrifice. One such religion was Moloch worship. It is condemned in various passages in 1 and 2 Kings. The sacrifice of children was the supreme sacrifice to the god Moloch.

Historically, cultures worldwide generally gave parents ultimate authority over their children. Infanticide played a role in such parental control. In China, India, Mexico, and Peru, children were cast into rivers in an effort to bring fine harvests and good fortune. In other early cultures the blood and flesh of slain infants was thought to confer vigor and health. As a result, it was fed to expectant mothers or favored siblings.[7]

Many cultures—not all primitive or ancient—have practiced forms of child mutilation for a variety of religious, medical, cosmetic, or economic reasons. Forms of mutilation such as gouged eyes, deformed feet, and amputated or twisted arms were inflicted on children in ancient Rome and later in England to evoke pity so they would be successful beggars.[8]

Too often, severe physical punishment of children has been permitted by parents and adults. For example, sick children were sometimes beaten for medical reasons to drive out demons thought to possess them. There are modern examples of this particular practice. In India epileptic children were thrashed with a sacred iron chain to expel the demon or demons.[9]

THE BREAK

Both Judaism and Christianity broke with the practice of other cultures and religions. True Christianity has always protested against the slaughter and misuse of children.

The early Christians preached against infanticide and exposure as murderous acts. In fact, the church became the place where mothers abandoned their children, knowing that the priest or pastor would place the children with someone in the parish.[10]

In the sixth century the European Christian orders began to provide asylums for abandoned children to combat the practices of exposure and infanticide. St. Vincent de Paul established his first children's institution after rescuing an infant from a beggar who was in the process of deforming its limbs.[11]

Even with certain lapses in history, such as occurred during the Middle Ages, the Christian concept of children as endowments from the Creator continued. This view of children was strongly resurrected in the parallel movements of the Renaissance and the Reformation. Moreover, the Reformation concept of children was carried forth by those who settled the new world.

THE INVENTION OF CHILDHOOD

It is difficult for those who live in contemporary society to see how sharp was the break with the past brought on by the Christian view of children. Christianity, in effect, "created" the modern concept and status of childhood—that is, children are not merely small adults.

Clear psychological evidence indicates that children "are not adults in miniature, they are being per se, different from their elders in their mental stature, their functioning, their understanding of events, and their reaction to them."[12] The basic fallacy of the children's liberation movement is their attempt to adultify children by, among other things, placing them on the same plane of activity as adults. This is neither realistic nor possible. In fact, it is harmful to children.

In today's society, however, everywhere one looks, it may be seen that the behavior, language, attitudes, and desires—even physical appearance—of adults and children are becoming increasingly indistinguishable. No doubt that is one reason why there exists a growing movement to recast the legal rights of children so that they are more or less the same as those of adults. The thrust of this movement resides in the claim that what has been thought to be a preferred status for children is instead only an oppression that keeps them from fully participating in society.

If we view the contemporary concern for the rights of children solely as a phenomenon of recent times and refuse to account for its historical underpinnings, we assume that the child has always held the same status as he does now in our society. We also assume that parents and society of other ages have had the same attitudes toward and expectations of the child as parents of this age. But historical evidence contradicts these assumptions.

> For example, the ten year old, whose behavior our schools, parents, and courts so carefully watch over and regulate, participated fully in the affairs of adults in the 1500s. There was no thought that a child of that age was either intellectually or physically incapable of performing these tasks.[13]

According to Philippe Ariès in his seminal work *Centuries of Childhood,* an awareness of the child as someone distinct and different from an adult was not an idea generally accepted until the seventeenth century.[14] An individual's life comprised but two broad periods: an extended "infancy," which lasted until six or seven years of age, and "adulthood."[15] High infant mortality rates and the short life span of adults were undoubtedly factors underlying the different attitude toward the infant and the early initiation of the young into the adult world.

When the child came to be viewed as an adult, he shared equally in the activities and responsibilities of the older adults. He was expected to and did work as other adults. He frequented the same places of entertainment, attended the same social gatherings, participated in the same games, and, if he could, read the same books.

The medieval child would have access to almost all of the forms of behavior common to the culture. The seven-year-old male was a man in every respect except for his capacity to make love and war.[16] "Certainly," J. H. Plumb writes, "there was no separate world of childhood. Children shared the same games with adults, the same toys, the same fairy stories. They lived their lives together, never apart. The coarse village festival depicted by Brueghel, showing men and women besotted with drink, groping for each other with unbridled lust, have children eating and drinking with the adults."[17]

Brueghel's paintings, in fact, show us two things at once: the inability and unwillingness of the culture to hide anything from children, and the absence of what became known in the sixteenth century as civilité, which is the other part. There did not exist a rich content of formal behavior for youth to learn. How impoverished that content was in the Middle Ages is difficult for modern civilization to grasp.

Erasmus, writing as late as 1523, gives us a vivid image of a German inn in his *Diversoria.* There are eighty to ninety people sitting together. They are of all social classes and all ages. Someone is washing clothes, which he hangs to dry on the stove. Another is cleaning his boots on the table. There is a common bowl for washing one's hands, but the water in it is filthy. The smell of garlic and other odors is everywhere. Spitting is frequent and unrestricted as to its destination. Everyone is sweating, for the room is overheated. Some wipe their noses on their clothing, and do not turn away when doing it. When the meal is brought in, each person dips his bread into the general dish, takes a bite, and dips again. There are no forks. Each takes the meat with his hands from the same dish, drinks wine from the same goblet, and sips soup from the same bowl.[18]

In order to understand how people could have endured this—indeed, not even noticed it—we must understand, as Norbert Elias reminds us, that "such people stood in a different relationship to one another than we do. And this involves not only the level of clear, rational consciousness; their emotional life also had a different structure and character."[19] Moreover, as Neil Postman notes, they did not have "the same concept of private space as we do; they were not repelled by certain human odors or bodily functions; they were not shamed by exposing their own bodily functions to the gaze of others; they felt no disgust in making contact with the hands and mouths of others."[20]

Considering this, we will not be surprised to know that in the Middle Ages there is no evidence for toilet training in the earliest months of the infant's life.[21] Or, as was the case, that there was no reluctance to discuss sexual matters in the presence of children. The idea of concealing sexual drives was alien to adults, and the idea of sheltering children from sexual secrets, unknown. As Ariès emphasizes: "Everything was permitted in their presence: coarse language, scabrous actions and situations; they had heard everything and seen everything."[22] Indeed, it was common enough in the Middle Ages for adults to take liberties with the sexual organs of children.

To the medieval mind such practices were merely ribald amusements. Again Ariès remarks: "The practice of playing with children's privy parts formed part of a widespread tradition."[23]

CHRISTIANITY

Fortunately for the medieval child, the church, as it did with other pagan practices directed against children, began protecting children:

> It was the religious pedagogues of the fifteenth and sixteenth centuries who first introduced and promulgated the idea of innocence. Because the influence of the Church

> was so extensive, its writings received considerable attention. The Church first took an interest in the child when it recognized the infant had an immortal soul.[24]

Thus, the idea that children need special care and protection was introduced into history.

Christianity thus made possible the break with the ancient pagan practices not only of infanticide and maiming, but also the use of children in what is now considered to be solely "adult" activities. William Barclay writes:

> No one owes more to Christianity than does the child. It is not that anyone would claim that even yet western civilization is fully Christian, but Christian principles have so permeated society that these things cannot happen in a society which has been touched by them.[25]

FIVE

THE BIBLICAL PATTERN

The two institutions offered as protective devices for the modern child are the family and the school.[1] However, the declining authority of the schools is well documented. Moreover, amid the radically changed nature of public schools from the educational to socializational function, they have become, as Marshall McLuhan once noted, houses of *detention* rather than *attention*.

Therefore, the only true safe harbor for children from the onslaught of modern culture is the family. Traditionally, the family was thought to be *the* only basic institution for communal life. It was not until the twentieth century that this assumption was challenged.

THE BASIC UNIT

There have in history been three types of family units: trustee, domestic, and atomistic. Unfortunately, some academicians such as Carle C. Zimmerman (an authority on the family and society) have viewed these three in evolutionary terms; that is, the trustee family as primitive and the atomistic as the product of a higher culture.[2]

Zimmerman posited that the *trustee* family is the basic authority and cohesive force in its society.[3] In the trustee family, the members are less important than the family. This family form, when it functions properly in a society, is the basic form of government for the people. Thus, it tends to limit the growth of the state. Moreover, what the family owns is in terms of property, and what it holds it passes on to generations to come. The trustee family tends to be patriarchal. But the head of the family represents, not his private wishes, but the religious, public, and social responsibilities of all members of the family.

The *domestic* family is one which has extensive powers, freedom, and social responsibilities; but the rise of a strong state has limited it. Legally, a significant difference is that title to the property is now vested in the man, the head of the household. As a consequence, the status of the wife declines because the husband now has more personal and arbitrary powers.

In the *atomistic* family, the family ceases to be the central unit. The individual becomes central and is the social value, not the family. The individual, as a result, is the social force. Family powers are steadily dissolved by statist laws, and the family is replaced by the state as the basic government.

Although all three family forms can exist within society, there has been a steady movement in contemporary society toward the atomistic model (with its emphasis on the individual and the state as the enforcer for the individual). Henry Maine, however, in his treatise *Ancient Law* (1861), demonstrates that ancient Western society began with a primary focus on the group, not the individual. According to Maine, the primal group was the family:

> [S]ociety in primitive times was not what it is assumed to be at present, a collection of *individuals*. In fact, and in the view of the men who composed it, *it was an aggregation of families*. The contrast may be most forcibly expressed by saying that the *unit* of an ancient society was the Family, of modern society the Individual.[4]

Maine further notes that "the movement of the progressive societies has been uniform in one respect."[5] He elaborates:

> Through all its course it has been distinguished by the gradual dissolution of family dependency and the growth of individual obligation in its place. The Individual is steadily substituted for the Family.[6]

The steady move from the trustee family to the individual tradition is reflected in such a modern phenomenon as the children's liberation movement. It is also reflected in the diminished influence of extended family kinship ties in today's highly mobile, industrialized society. It has come to the point where it can be said that in a large segment of society there are families only in form, not content. And if in a particular situation a family does exist, who has control? Is it the parent, the children, or the state?

THE BIBLICAL TRADITION

The family is in some ways a uniquely Biblical institution. In fact, it is specifically ordained of God in the book of Genesis.[7]

By using the Bible to answer the question of who is in authority over the children (the state or the family), the question is put into an absolute framework. In the Bible, the Creator's truths are fixed, uniform, and universal. They are not judged by a balancing test, screened for viability, or weighed in terms of pleasure against pain. The Creator's principles *are,* just as the Creator *is*.

Moreover, the Bible views all institutions, including civil government and the family, in terms of the same basic authority. It is *derivative* authority from God. It is *delegated* to human beings from God. But it is always seen in relation to the Creator and the revealed will of the Creator.

The Bible also explains that God has distinguished between certain groups or institutions by giving them diverse authority and duties. The church's purpose is different from the civil government's, which is again different from the family's. Therefore, the first question is: to which group did God give the oversight and care of children?

Children have been important since the beginning. The crowning work of creation was human beings, both man and woman. Children, thus, are mentioned very early in the Bible.[8] There Adam and Eve were told to be fruitful and multiply.

Not only is there a command to have children, but there is the teaching that children are from God. When Eve had borne a child, she recognized that she had not done this alone and understood that the Creator was the ultimate source of the child. She said: "I have gotten a man from the Lord."[9]

In Genesis 33:5 Jacob tells Esau that the children he sees are "the children whom God has graciously given your servant." Joseph told his father, Israel, that "they are my sons, whom God has given me here."[10] The Creator spoke to His people and said: "Then I took your father Abraham from beyond the River, and led him through all the land of Canaan, and multiplied his descendants and gave him Isaac. And to Isaac I gave Jacob and Esau."[11]

These verses indicate that children are given by God to families and not inanimate institutions or governments. Not only are children given, but they are also called gifts and blessings: "Behold, children are a gift of the Lord; the fruit of the womb is a reward."[12] As such, children are not just given to any family. The implication is that specific children are given to particular parents as a gift from God.

In this light it would be necessary to question if infants are the result of a simply biological function, as the state and its courts believe, or as a personal reward from the Creator. Jeremiah states: "Before I formed you in the womb I knew you, and before you were born I consecrated you."[13] Thus, the Bible states children are created by God and are gifts entrusted by God to families.

The family was the first institution created by God, even before the state. Because it was the first, it can be considered to be the foundational institution upon which all others are built. It is within the family that children learn how to worship God and how to be effective and productive citizens.

The Biblical family is patriarchal. The father is, thus, the leader of the family—but in the sense of the trustee family and not in the autocracy of other family forms.

In Genesis 9:1-17, God entered into a covenant with Noah, the head of his family. In Job 1:5, Job intercedes in prayer that God would protect his family. In Genesis 27, Isaac blessed his sons. In these activities—blessing, interceding, covenanting—the father is God's representative within the family.

As we have seen, this patriarchal design does not fit well within a modern egalitarian society. As a consequence, conflicts with the state are inevitable. However, this does not negate the fact that the Creator has given the primary authority over children to the family.

RESPONSIBILITY

Parenthood requires a responsibility to handle the gift of children properly. This means that parents must perform specific duties toward their children. These duties stem from their derivative authority—derivative of the Creator.

The first duty is *provision* of a child's basic needs. The Apostle Paul wrote: "For children are not responsible to save up for their parents, but parents for their children."[14] Again, Paul said: "But if anyone does not provide for his own, and especially for those of his household he has denied the faith, and is worse than an unbeliever."[15]

The second duty is *protection* of the children. Paul writes: "But we proved to be gentle among you, as a nursing mother tenderly cares for her own children."[16]

In this respect, Christ's teachings concerning children (and women) is one of the true break-points in history. Christ's conception of children, in general, departed from the chattel-mentality of his time. This included His disciples.

For example, we are told: "Then were there brought unto him little children, that he should put his hands on them, and pray: and *the disciples rebuked them.*"[17] However, Christ replied: "Suffer [allow] little children, and forbid them not, to come unto me: for of such is the kingdom of heaven."[18] Then Christ "laid his hands on them, and departed thence."[19]

Two immediate principles are taught in this passage. First, children are distinct from adults. A concept of childhood is asserted here. But also, as distinct human beings, children possess a worth and dignity apart from adults. Christ even presents children as the example of what it means to be a true believer.[20]

Second, as children they need special protection because they are special beings.[21] That is the partial significance of Christ laying His hands on and blessing the children. Thus, they must be cared for.[22]

In the book of Hebrews we read: "By faith Moses, when he was born, was hidden for three months by his parents, because they saw he was a beautiful child; and they were not afraid of the King's edict."[23] According to God's law, then, protecting the child's life is one of the parents' basic duties. The Bible makes no exceptions for sex, intellect, or for pre- or postnatal children. Moses' parents risked their lives in order to save him. That is the Biblical mandate for parental protection.

Correction and discipline is a duty the neglect of which harms a child. As Hebrews instructs: "But if you are without discipline, of which we all have been partakers, then you are illegitimate children and not sons."[24] If one does correct his children, he will be honored by them: "Furthermore, we had earthly fathers to discipline us, and we respected them."[25]

However, *all* discipline should be carried forth with love and compassion for the child: "And, fathers, do not provoke your children to anger; but bring them up in the discipline and instruction of the Lord."[26] If not, parents could commit criminal acts against their children. In such a case, the state, in serving its proper function, has an arguable interest in protecting children.

Training is another important duty of the parents, for it shapes a child as surely as pruning does a tree. Proverbs states: "Train a child up in the way he should go, even when he is old he will not depart from it."[27] Deuteronomy likewise stresses proper training of children: "And these words, which I am commanding you today, shall be on your heart; and you shall teach them diligently to your sons and shall talk of them when you sit in your house and when you walk by the way and when you lie down and when you rise up."[28] Training, however, is more than providing children with information. It is working moral precepts into their characters.

EDUCATION

A major duty for parents is the *education* of their children. "Only give heed to yourself and keep your soul diligently," the book of Deuteronomy reads, "lest you forget the things which your eyes have seen, and lest they depart from your heart all the days of your life; but make them known to your sons and your grandsons."[29]

The duties of education, training, correction, protection, and provision are outlined in the Bible so that parents know what they must do and what they must prevent the state and others from doing. Therefore, because children are given as *rewards,* they are to be reared on "all scripture [which] is inspired by God and profitable for teaching, for reproof, for correction, for training in righteousness that the man of God may be adequate, equipped for every good work."[30]

Instruction in Christian principles, however, is not intended to produce automatons. Instead, it is intended to create a moral consciousness in children so that they will be more productive people.

In the area of education the Bible lists several options for education, but none of them replace or overrule the parents. The *parents* are the first and main teachers. They also are responsible to supervise any outside instruction the children may receive.

In Old Testament Israel there were no schools for the average child. Boys were taught a trade by their fathers, and parents instructed all their children in the law and religious festivals. By the time of Jesus Christ, boys went to school at the age of six. The schools were attached to the synagogue. Here the priests would instruct the students in the law. At the age of thirteen the boys became "Bar Mitzvah" or a son of the new law.

It was, however, the responsibility of the parents to fulfill the instruction of religious festivals and to teach their sons a trade. The religious instruction was left at home and in the synagogue, for the teaching of the law was made distinct from the religious customs.

The conclusion is obvious: in God's plan, the primary responsibility for educating the young lies in the home and directly in the father. The family, then, is man's first and basic school. In fact, parents will have extensively educated their children before the child ever sets foot inside an institutional school. Every mother regularly performs the most difficult of all educational tasks, one which no school performs. For instance, the mother takes a small child, incapable of speaking or understanding a word in any language, and teaches the child to speak. This is, of course, a difficult task.

Basic education of the child is painstaking, but it comes naturally in a family as an expression of the mother's love. At every stage of the child's life, the educational function of the home should be the basic educational power in the life of the child.

In fact, the family is where the child first learns religion, government (hopefully, self-government), and a wide range of subjects currently thought to be the sole province of state schools. The family, then, is the primary health, education, and welfare institution of society.

Granted that the family, in Biblical terms, possesses the basic function of education, the question is: Can that function be *delegated* to other persons or, for that matter, to other institutions?

The family's educational function was delegated to the Levitical priesthood in old Israel.[31] This was also true in Christ's day. Moreover, in the early church the educational function was delegated to church leaders. As such, the church is the Creator's other primary teaching institution (other than the family).

This delegation, however, must be in accordance with Scripture: "The fear of the Lord is the beginning of knowledge."[32] Any delegation, therefore, to a person or institution that is not grounded in the Word of God is contrary to the Creator's purpose.

Since there is no reference in Scripture to the school as a separate institution from the family, a truly Biblical school must be an extension of the family. The school must function *in loco parentis* (that is, in place of the parent). A legitimate school, therefore, should stand in the stead of the parent and should reflect and teach only those Christian values and ideas which tend to strengthen the family.

INTO THE FABRIC

Various cultures have attempted to place a Biblical design for the family into their societal fabric. Where it has been so placed, it has had dramatic effects. One such culture affected was America. It is here that the European Reformation may have had its greatest effect.

SIX

THE AMERICAN EXPERIENCE

The founding of America was quite unique in that it was seen as a religious experience. The Mayflower Compact of November 11, 1620 proclaims:

> Having undertaken for the Glory of God, and Advancement of the Christian Faith, and the Honour of our King and Country, a Voyage to plant the first colony . . . Do by these Presents, solemnly and mutually in the Presence of God and one another, covenant and combine ourselves together into a civil Body Politick.[1]

Religion to many of the early American settlers was a total reality—unlike the fragmented religion of modern Christianity. Their religion was something upon which they structured every aspect of their existence.

THE PURITANS

The totality of religious experience was especially true of the Puritans and their views on the family and parental authority. Although the Puritans have been maligned by some contemporary writers, it is now evident that their impact on American society has been considerable.[2]

The Puritans, who were prominent in New England in the sixteenth and seventeenth century, regarded the family as a sacred and vitally important institution.[3] Indeed, the maintaining of proper relationships between husband and wife, and parent and child, were seen as crucial for their very survival.[4] Children were required to submit to the authority of their parents. The family relationship was understood to have been instituted by God. The husband was seen as the head of the household.[5]

These relationships were zealously guarded and maintained as "the very ligaments by which society was held together—'the root whence church and commonwealth cometh.' "[6] An adopted maxim of the day was that "families are the nurseries of church and commonwealth; ruin families and you ruin all."[7]

The history of the early colonial period, in fact, supports this belief in the vital role of the family. As historian Arthur Calhoun points out, the success of the American colonies, in contrast to those of the French and Spanish, was largely due to the fact that they came "not as individual adventurers, but as families."[8]

The Puritans, however, did not base their high regard for the family on mere practical considerations. To them it was an aspect of obedience to God.[9] The Bible was the single most important influence in their lives,[10] and their understanding of proper family order and government was founded upon the Scriptures and seen as ordained by God.[11]

Parental authority, then, was understood to be God-given authority. Similarly, the duties and responsibilities of parents to their children were, in their minds, established and commanded by God.[12]

The proper devotional literature of Puritan New England, which had wide circulation at that time, reflects this same reverence for the family institution. These works, such as John Dod's *A Godly Forme of Household Government* and Rev. William Gauge's *Of Domestic Duties,* portray the family as the microcosm of state, church, and school, righteously ruled by the father as head of the household.[13]

Training, educating, and bringing up one's children was the sacred right and duty of parents. The corresponding duty of children was to obey cheerfully and reverently, heeding their parent's instruction and emulating their good examples.[14] All of these views were thoroughly supported with Scripture references[15] and constantly reinforced in sermons.[16]

HOME AND EDUCATION

To the Puritan and Pilgrim of early America, the family home or household was not only cherished as a "preeminent treasure."[17] It was central in their lives.

As the historian Lawrence Cremin notes, the early New England colonists believed in and consistently maintained "the centrality of the household as the primary agency of human association and education."[18] Cremin further describes the family as "the principal unit of social organization in the colonies and the most important agency of popular education."[19] This was not due to a lack of alternative means, nor to isolation. Cremin explains:

> There were ample opportunities for social intercourse among the members of different families and for joint sponsorship of readily accessible churches and schools. . . . It was ideology rather than geography that established the primacy of the household; for the Puritans considered the family the basic unit of church and commonwealth and, ultimately, the nursery of sainthood.[20]

In the Puritan household, children received a good deal of sustained and systematic instruction.[21] Parents were deeply concerned that their children receive an education in order that they might understand the Bible and Christian doctrine.[22]

Indeed, to the Puritan mind, learning and godliness were inseparably linked. The Bible was frequently used as a reading text. Catechisms were learned to insure that the Scriptures would be interpreted and applied properly.[23] In addition to obtaining an understanding of the Bible, the chief concern of education was in building up godly, moral character in the child for "the practice of true piety."[24]

Even though the primary emphasis of Puritan education was religious, children were still generally taught and learned "the three R's."[25] Children were thus instilled with religious and moral training, and were taught how to read and write at a very early age—even by today's standards.[26]

Furthermore, Purtain parents, in preparing and educating their children for adult life, also instructed them in a "lawful" calling or occupation.[27] This home-centered and parent-supervised education system, as Arthur Calhoun recognizes, was effective:

> The colonial home was a little world . . . under whose roof the children could, if need were, learn all that was necessary for their future careers. The Puritans, as has been seen, were strong for the training of children for their duties here and beyond.[28]

Not all the parents of Puritan New England, though, were capable of teaching their children reading and writing. To aid parents in fulfilling their important responsibilities,[29] the Massachusetts Bay Colony enacted the School Law of 1647 (commonly called "The Old Deluder Act"). In order to prevent that "old deluder Satan" from keeping men "from the knowledge of ye Scriptures," and "learning may not be buried in ye grave of our fathers," it was ordered that a school be established in every town of over fifty households, with the teacher being paid wages by the parents of those children who used the school.[30] And in towns of over 100 households they also "shall set up a grammar schoole," in order to "instruct youth so farr as they shall be fitted for ye university."[31] Because the duty to provide and direct the child's education was seen as completely under the authority of parents, attendance at such schools was on a purely *voluntary* basis.[32]

There were, then, a number of educational options available for parents, even if they were unable to personally conduct the teaching of their children. Moreover, even with the establishment of town schools, households were so prominently involved in the education process that it was often difficult to distinguish "home" from "school." Arthur Cremin describes this fact of seventeenth-century colonial life:

> For youngsters growing up in homes in which no one was equipped to teach reading, there was frequently a neighborhood household where they might acquire the skill. And, indeed, when an occasional New England goodwife decided to teach reading in her kitchen and charge a modest fee, she thereby became a "dame school," or when an

occasional Virginia family decided to have a servant (or tutor) undertake the task of its own and perhaps some neighbor's children, the servant became a "petty school." Such enterprises were schools, to be sure, but they were also household activities, and the easy shading of one into the other is a significant educational fact of the seventeenth century.[33]

LAW AND PARENTAL AUTHORITY

In the Puritan colonies, the state was to be guided by the church and the Scriptures.[34] It was to be a "Godly commonwealth"[35] which punished evil and strengthened and encouraged the good.[36] Thus, with the Puritans' deep concern for the welfare of the family and for maintaining proper family relationships, it naturally followed that from the outset the colonly leaders promoted family life.

Of special concern to the Puritan leaders, though, was the maintaining of parental authority.[37] The very well-being of the community was conceived to depend upon family order and discipline.[38] As such, in every household children were brought up and trained to render respect and obedience to parents, with strict punishment often imposed for disobedience.[39]

Recognizing the inherent dangers which could result from impairment of parental authority, Puritan lawmakers passed a variety of laws designed to strengthen and reinforce that authority, backing up parents with the sanctions of the state.[40] It is at this point that modern child-rearing philosophy is in dire conflict with Puritan views.

For example, in the Massachusetts Act of 1654, magistrates were permitted to have children taken out and whipped for acts of rebellion and disobedience against their parents.[41] The language of this law reflects the great concern to uphold stable family life and parental authority:

> Forasmuch as it appeareth by too much experience, that diverse children and servants do behave themselves disobediently and disorderly towards their parents, masters and governors . . . to the disturbance of families, and discouragement of such parents and governors.[42]

Perhaps the harshest law of this sort is the 1648 enactment which permitted the death penalty in the case of a persistently rebellious and disobedient son, or where a child cursed or struck a parent.[43] This law, based upon passages from the Old Testament, gave parents the right to petition the court for the imposition of this punishment—but *there is no evidence that any parent ever did so, and the law was apparently never invoked.*[44]

Nevertheless, the mere fact that these offenses against parental authority were listed among the fifteen "capitall lawes" clearly indicates the great respect and reverence which the Puritans held for that authority. The actual language of the laws is instructive of this fact:

> 13. If any child, or children, above sixteen years old, and of sufficient understanding, shall CURSE, or SMITE their natural FATHER, or MOTHER: he or they shall be put to death: unless it can be sufficiently testified that the Parents have been very unchristianly negligent in the education of such children; or so provoked them by extream, and cruel correction; that they have been forced thereunto to preserve themselves from death or maiming. Exod. 21.17, Lev. 20.9, Exod. 21.15.
>
> 14. If a man have a stubborn or REBELLIOUS SON, of sufficient years and understanding (viz) fifteen years of age, which will not obey the voice of his Father, or the voice of his Mother, and that when they have chastened him will not harken unto them: then shall his Father & Mother being his natural parents, lay hold on him, and bring him to the Magistrates and assembled in court and testify unto them, that their Son is stubborn & rebellious & will not obey their voice and chastisement, but lives in sundry notorious crimes, such a Son shall be put to death. Deut. 21, 20.21.[45]

The importance attached to parental authority and discipline is further illustrated by the fact that the courts often sent youthful offenders to their families for parental correction and punishment.[46] Pursuant to this policy, Massachusetts ordered in 1645 that, as to such child lawbreakers, "parents or masters shall give them due correction and that in the presence of some officer if any magistrate shall appoint."[47]

Other notable laws respecting parental authority include one which forbade tailors from fashioning garments for children which were "contrary to the mind and order of their parents."[48] There was also a law requiring parental approval for a child to marry. This law, however, was tempered by the fact that parents could not "unreasonably deny any childe timely or convenient marriage."[49]

Parental authority carried with it great responsibility. Puritan leaders were, therefore, very concerned that the duties of parents were not being neglected, particularly in the area of education.[50] In 1642, the Massachusetts Bay Colony enacted America's first compulsory education law, providing that "because of the great neglect of many parents & masters in training up their children," men be chosen in every town who would "take account from time to time of all parents" to see to it that their children were able to "read and understand the principles of religion and the capitall lawes of this country."[51] A penalty of twelve shillings was imposed for each instance of neglect in this area.[52] By 1648, the law specified more clearly what was required of parents:

> The Selectmen of everie town . . . shall have a vigilant eye over their bretheren and neighbors, to see, first that none of them shall suffer so much barbarism in any of their families as not to endeavor to teach by themselves or others, their children and apprentices so much learning as may enable them perfectly to read the english tongue, & knowledge of the capitall lawes. . . . Also that all masters of families doe once a week (at the least) catechize their children and servants in the grounds and principles of Religion.[53]

These statutes, Cremin notes, by and large merely compelled parents to do what they had been accustomed to doing all along.[54] Parents were being directed by law to fulfill their duty to educate their children, a traditional responsibility of parents in the Christian family.[55]

The other New England colonies soon followed the lead of Massachusetts Bay. In 1650, Connecticut required that children be taught to read English, instructed in the capital laws, and catechized weekly.[56] New Haven followed suit in 1655, New York in 1665, and Plymouth in 1671.[57] In 1665, a Connecticut law admonished that the reading of Scripture and the catechizing of children was a responsibility of "every Christian family," and the neglect of it a great sin.[58] And, in 1683, an ordinance of the new colony of Pennsylvania provided that all parents and guardians of children "shall cause such to be instructed in reading and writing, so that they may be able to read the Scriptures and to write by the time they attain to twelve years of age."[59]

All of these enactments were concerned simply with the basic education of children, and should not, therefore, be confused with modern compulsory education laws which require classroom attendance at state-approved schools.[60] The responsibility for the child's education in New England (and the rest of the colonies which had no such statutes) was left solely with the parents.[61] Moreover, the power of town ministers or "selectmen" to investigate such matters of family life was quickly curtailed in these colonies by the growing acceptance of the idea that every family's household was personal. That is, the common-law principle that "every man's home is his castle" was respected.[62]

By the last quarter of the seventeenth century there was a rapid decline in interest, or growing dislike, for the idea of compulsory education.[63] The laws were substantially weakened or qualified and then repealed outright, so that by the eighteenth century there were no longer any laws requiring compulsory education in New England.[64]

A suggested cause for this trend is the dilution of Puritan strength and the increasing religious toleration between the various Christian sects.[65] Also, the importance of religion had diminished among the colonists, thus depriving the compulsory education laws of their basic reason for existing—religious instruction.[66] In any event, it was not until well after the Revolution that interest in such laws returned.[67]

HEALTH, EDUCATION AND WELFARE

Evidently the Puritans viewed the family as *the* health, education, and welfare institution of society. These three concerns were seen as private functions to be administered in and through the family.

As we have seen in our times, when the state assumes these functions, the health, education, and welfare of the citizenry decline. The state is simply, and will always be, a poor and ineffective parental substitute.

SEVEN

THE EARLY AMERICAN FAMILY

A basic characteristic of early American society—one diametrically opposed to the modern concept of the family—was the family's *centrality* in the culture. It was as if the family was the center of the wheel of society with all the other institutions being mere spokes. Preeminent in all this was parental authority.

EIGHTEENTH-CENTURY AMERICA

The firm belief in the sacredness and importance of the family continued unchallenged through eighteenth and early nineteenth century America.[1] Life was, as it had been from the Puritan beginnings, home-centered, with parental authority over children reigning unopposed.[2] This was true of the southern colonies as well as of those in the north.[3] The colonists of this period were, therefore, heirs to the tradition which "stressed the centrality of the household as the primary agency of human association and education."[4]

To be sure, there were many changes in colonial life during the eighteenth and early nineteenth century. The population increased substantially. More and more new towns were established, while the older ones were built up and improved. Survival was less of a hardship, and life expectancy increased. Commerce and enterprise were beginning to flourish. Finally, the number of churches and schools increased dramatically as well, making them even more accessible to colonial families.[5]

In addition to these changes, religious toleration of all the various Christian sects was becoming the predominant view. Also, more representative forms of government were emerging out of the Puritan governments. Arthur Calhoun states that in all this change, the "family was the one substantial institution in a nation that had discarded hierarchical religion and that reduced government to a minimum."[6]

Through all of these changes the family remained a constant, maintaining its important role and continuing to fulfill its traditional duties and responsibilities.[7] Lawrence Cremin describes this reality of eighteenth-century American life:

> The household remained the single most fundamental unit of social organization in the eighteenth century colonies and, for the vast majority of Americans, the decisive agency of deliberate cultural transmission. In frontier regions marked by a pattern of dispersed settlement, it continued to educate much as it had in the early years of the middle and southern plantations, taking unto itself functions ordinarily performed by church and school. And, in the older, more settled regions, even as churches became more numerous, schools more accessible, and hamlets more common, it continued to discharge its traditional obligations for the systematic nurture of piety, civility and learning.[8]

The family also retained its function as the primary health, education, and welfare institution of society. Again Cremin recounts:

> In the beginning was the family. In the Christian West, it was traditionally monogamous, patriarchal, and, at least until the early modern era, inclusive of other than blood relatives. It provided food and clothing, succor and shelter; it conferred social standing, economic possibility, and religious affiliation; and it served from time to time as church, playground, factory, army and court. In addition, it was almost always a school, proffering to the young their earliest ideas about the nature of the world and how one ought to behave in it.[9]

In sum, as Cremin notes, "families did more and taught more, in a process of nurturing a versatility in the young that was highly significant for the development of colonial society."[10]

COLONIAL EDUCATION

Parents, of course, still had sole authority and control over the education of their children in colonial America. Although schools greatly increased in importance as a source of education, the home or family remained steadfast as a primary source of all instruction and training.[11]

The general consensus was that education was "the concern of the individual family" and "the private function of the parent, with any state interference unjustified in terms of individual rights."[12] As a result, state involvement was generally limited to providing for the education of indigent children. As Cremin notes:

> The community, acting through philanthropic agencies, religious agencies, or the state, took an interest only at points where a spirit of Christian charity impelled them to provide it for the poor.[13]

Thus, from the founding of the original colonies of Puritan New England until the early years following the adoption of the Constitution, home education was one of the major forms, if not the predominant form, of education.[14]

Indeed, many of the framers of the American founding documents received all or a substantial part of their education in the home. This includes George Washington,[15] Thomas Jefferson,[16] Patrick Henry,[17] James Madison,[18] and Benjamin Franklin.[19]

In a letter on the subject of education written by George Washington, he expresses his belief that it is the personal duty of a parent or guardian to provide a child's education. In this letter, Washington states why his ward (son-in-law) is not yet ready for marriage, but also reveals his view of where the responsibility of education rests:

> [H]is youth, inexperience, and unripened education, is, and will be insuperable obstacles in my eye, to the completion of the marriage. As his guardian, I conceive it to be my indispensable duty to carry him through a regular course of education . . . and to guard his youth to a more advanced age.[20]

Earlier in the eighteenth century, Cotton Mather, Puritan scholar, clergyman, and author, had described in detail the methods of instruction he used in educating his children at home. The description he gives us may be regarded as characteristic of the time.[21] He wrote as follows:

Some Special Points, Relating to the Education of My Children

I. I pour out continual prayers and cries to the God of all grace for them, that he will be a father to my children, and bestow his Christ and his grace upon them, and guide them with his counsels, and bring them to his glory.

And in this action, I mention them distinctly, every one by name unto the Lord.

II. I begin betimes to entertain them with delightful stories, especially Scriptural ones. And still conclude with some lesson of piety; bidding them to learn that lesson from the story.

And thus, every day at the table, I have used myself to tell a story before I rise; and made the story useful to the olive plants about the table.

III. When the children at any time accidently come in my way, it is my custom to let fall some sentence or other, that may be monitory and profitable to them.

This matter proves to me, a matter of some study, and labor, and contrivance. But who can tell, what may be the effect of a continual dropping?

IV. I essay betimes, to engage the children, in exercises of piety; and especially secret prayer, for which I give them very plain and brief directions, and suggest unto them the petitions, which I would have them to make before the Lord, and which I therefore explain to their apprehension and capacity. And I often call upon them; Child, don't you forget every day, to go alone, and pray as I have directed you!

V. Betimes I try to form in the children a temper of benignity. I put them upon doing of services and kindnesses for one another, and for other children. I applaud them, when I see them delight in it. I upbraid all aversion to it. I caution them exquisitely against all revenges of injuries. I instruct them, to return good offices for evil ones. I show them, how they will by this goodness become like to the good God, and his glorious Christ. I let them discern, that I am not satisfied, except when they have a sweetness of temper shining in them.

VI. As soon as 'tis possible, I make the children learn to write. And when they can write, I employ them in writing out the most agreeable and profitable things, that I can invent for them. In this way, I propose to freight their minds with excellent things, and have a deep impression made upon their minds by such things.

VII. I mightily endeavor it, that the children may betimes, be acted by principles of reason and honor.

I first beget in them a high opinion of their father's love to them, and of his being best able to judge, what shall be good for them.

Then I make them sensible, 'tis a folly for them to pretent unto any wit and will of their own; they must resign all to me, and will be sure to do what is best; my word must be their law.

I cause them to understand, that it is a hurtful and a shameful thing to do amiss. I aggravate this, on all occasions; and let them see how amiable they will render themselves by well-doing.

The first chastisement, which I inflict for an ordinary fault, is, to let the child see and hear me in an astonishment, and hardly able to believe that the child could do so base a thing, but believing that they will never do it again.

I would never come, to give a child a blow; except in case of obstinacy: or some gross enormity.

To be chased for a while out of my presence, I would make to be looked upon, as the sorest punishment in the family.

I would by all possible insinuations gain this point upon them, that for them to learn all the brave things in the world, is the bravest thing in the world. I am not found of proposing play to them, as a reward of any diligent application to learn what is good; lest they should think diversion to be a better and a nobler thing than diligence.

I would have them come to propound and expect, at this rate, *I have done well, and now I will go to my father; he will teach me some curious thing for it*. I must have them count it a privilege, to be taught; and I sometimes manage the matter so, that my refusing to teach them something, is their punishment.

The slavish way of education, carried on with raving and kicking and scourging (in schools as well as families), 'tis abominable; and a dreadful judgment of God upon the world.

VIII. Though I find it a marvelous advantage to have the children strongly biased by principles of reason and honor, (which, I find, children will feel sooner than is commonly thought for): yet I would neglect no endeavors, to have higher principles infused into them.

I therefore betimes awe them with the eye of God upon them.

I show them, how they must love Jesus Christ, and show it, by doing what their parents require of them.

I often tell them of the good angels, who love them, and help them, and guard them; and who take notice of them: and therefore must not be disobliged.

Heaven and hell, I set before them, as the consequences of their behavior here.

IX. When the children are capable of it, I take them alone, one by one; and after my charges unto them, to fear God, and serve Christ, and shun sin, I pray with them in my study and make them the witnesses of the agonies, with which I address the Throne of Grace on their behalf.

X. I find much benefit, by a particular method, as of catechizing the children, so of carrying the repetition of the public sermons unto them.

The answers of the catechism I still explain with abundance of brief questions, which make them to take in the meaning of it, and I see, that they do so.

And when the sermons are to be repeated, I choose to put every truth, into a question, to be answered still, with, yes, or, no. In this way I awaken their attention, as well as enlighten their understanding. And in this way I have an opportunity, to ask, *Do you desire such, or such a grace of God?* and the like. Yea, I have an opportunity to demand, and perhaps, to obtain their consent unto the glorious articles of the new covenant. The spirit of grace may fall upon them in this action; and they may be seized by him, and held as his temples, through eternal ages.[22]

Summing up the important role of the family as a source of education during this period in our history, Cremin writes:

> [A] great deal of formal and informal education, intellectual, technical, attitudinal, continued to take place, with the young learning mostly by imitation and partly through explanation. Reading was still taught in the home by parents and siblings, from hornbooks, catechisms, primers, and Bibles, and, as a matter of fact the common expectation that books would be read aloud in the household is probably the single most important clue to the particular stylistic approach of a good deal of early popular literature—such as was certainly the case with the novels of Samuel Richardson, *The Family Instructor* (1915) of Daniel Defoe, and the essays of Addison and Steele.[23]

And not only were basic skills and trades taught, but also "the values and behaviors associated with piety and civility were systematically nurtured."[24]

An additional distinguishing feature of eighteenth-century colonial education was the great "diversity of alternatives" available to parents in fulfilling their responsibility of educating their children.[25] Whether in households, churches, schools, or a combination of these, the means of acquiring an education became both more accessible and more diverse.[26] Moreover, in deciding among these various alternatives, parents had absolute discretion and authority. As one commentator notes:

> Historically, the education of children in the United States was a matter of parental discretion. Decisions to educate or not to educate, and the substance of that education—method and curriculum—were made by the parents as a right.[27]

THE FRAMERS

The success of this manner of education—that is, parental control among a diversity of alternatives, including home education—was quite remarkable. It helped produce one of the most extraordinary generations of leaders and statesmen in history, well-prepared for the founding of a new nation.[28] It is instructive to note that among the signers of the Declaration of Independence were represented, in terms of education, every conceivable combination of parental, church, apprenticeship, school, tutorial, and self-education, including some who had studied abroad.[29]

Besides the quality of the leadership, another indication of the success of eighteenth-century education was the remarkable degree of literacy. At the time of the Revolution, literacy rates had reached unprecedented heights,[30] and by 1800 literacy was virtually universal.[31]

The general education of the populace was such a well-known fact of life that Thomas Jefferson could unabashedly extol the wisdom of the people "without ultimately sounding like a fool."[32] Commenting on this striking degree of literacy and learning throughout the colonies, John Adams stated in 1765:

> [A] native of America who cannot read or write is as rare an appearance . . . as a comet or an earthquake.[33]

He later said:

> I have good authority to say, that all foreigners who have passed through this country, and conversed freely with all sorts of people here, will allow, that they have never seen so much knowledge and civility among the common people in any part of the world.[34]

Furthermore, what the colonists were able to achieve in the area of education also made quite an impact on Europe. Cremin writes:

> In 1689, the question in the minds of most Europeans was whether North America was yet sufficiently civilized for habitation. A century later, the question was rather what Europe could learn from America: a new education in a new land had wrought new men who seemed to hold the future in their hands.[35]

It is important to note that the education progress in early America was essentially the result of family-oriented education. And although the framers believed education was to be encouraged and promoted, *it was not to be compelled.* Compulsion in education, it was believed, could result in depriving parents of control over their children.

Thomas Jefferson squarely rejected the notion of compulsion in the area of education in upholding the rights of parents. He said:

> It is better to tolerate the rare instance of a parent refusing to let his child be educated, than to shock the common feelings and ideas by the forcible asportation and education of the infant against the will of the father.[36]

In other words, education, no matter how important to the well-being of the nation, was not to be placed above parental rights and traditional family morality. Thus, even though Jefferson was for the formation of some form of public education, he never questioned the fundamental role of the family in the education of children.[37]

Other leaders and writers had a strongly felt influence in the field of education in colonial America. One popular work throughout the colonies was John Locke's *Some Thoughts Concerning Education.*[38] Locke advised all parents, in teaching their children, to begin early in the child's development with the Lord's Prayer, the creeds, and the Decalogue. This was to be followed with instruction in reading in following the "ordinary road of the hornbook, primer, Psalter, Testament and Bible."[39] Moreover, parents were to insure that the Bible itself was systematically studied as the foundation of all morality.[40]

Another influential leader in the field of American education was John Witherspoon, a Presbyterian minister and president of Princeton University. His students reached positions of eminence in early America. They included a president, a vice-president, ten cabinet members, sixty members of Congress, and three Justices of the Supreme Court.[41] Witherspoon also was one of the signers of the Declaration of Independence.[42] In his letters on education, Witherspoon stressed the great necessity for parents "to establish as soon as possible, an entire and absolute authority" over their children.[43]

THE FIRST CONGRESS

This concern for traditional morality and family values was also reflected in the laws passed by the early Congresses. For instance, according to the Northwest Territory Code of 1788, children who disobeyed their parents might, on approval of a justice of the peace in that territory, be sent for a brief stay in jail until, as the law put it, they were "humbled."[44] And the Northwest Ordinance of 1789, which provided the guidelines for the establishing of governments in the territories, also set forth the priorities of the day:

> Religion, morality, and knowledge, being necessary to good government and the happiness of mankind, schools and the means of education shall forever be encouraged.[45]

This clearly expresses the intent of the first Congress to maintain religion and traditional morality within the framework of the educational process, which at that time was essentially a family function.

THE WORKMANSHIP OF THE MAKER

It was during the eighteenth century that certain Enlightenment writers were articulating the nature of children and their relationship to their parents and society. One such writer, John Locke, attempted to put it in a Christian context.[46]

In his *Second Treatise of Government* (1691), Locke characterizes the relationship between parent and child as follows:

> Adam was created a perfect man, his body and mind in full possession of their strength and reason, and so was capable from the first instant of his being to provide for his own support and preservation and govern his actions according to the dictates of the law of reason which God had implanted in him. From him the world is peopled with his descendants who are all born infants, weak and helpless, without knowledge or understanding; but to supply the defects of this imperfect state till the improvement of growth and age has removed them. Adam and Eve, and after them all parents, were by the law of nature "under an obligation to preserve, nourish, and educate the children" they had begotten; not as their own workmanship, but the workmanship of their own Maker, the Almighty, to whom they were to be accountable for them.[47]

This passage advocates certain basic principles that place the child within a Christian perspective. As a preface to discussing these principles, it is emphasized that eighteenth-century spirituality saw God's work as the creation of an orderly, well-governed universe in which independent parts were in harmony with all others. As such, God's children were destined to take their place in the moral social order as well-developed adults.

First, as Locke articulated, children are not merely the property of their parents. They are the creation of God. Therefore, instead of belonging to their parents, children belong to the Creator. Parents, then, hold children in trust for God. This means that parents, as stewards, are to take care of their children for *God.* The child must be raised to live the sort of life which is pleasing to the Creator. Locke says this is in accordance with the "dictates of the law of reason." As such, it is a primary moral and spiritual function of the family.

Second, although children lack total adult human capacities, they do not lack humanity. Locke notes that children are "weak and helpless, without knowledge or understanding." In short, children do not yet have what is required to be a being pleasing to the Creator. At an early age they do not yet have the mental and moral development to enable them to live under the "law of reason." They are in need of care.

As potential independent beings, children, Locke reasons, are born *to* a state of equality, but not *in* a state of equality. Not only does this emphasize that children have a life of their own to live someday, but that things can turn out well or badly. There are no guarantees that the weak infant will become the reasoning adult. Parents, thus, have a moral duty to take steps to see that the "improvement of growth and age" actually come about in producing independent adults.

Third, the child's weakness is a source of parental authority, which in turn is a source of parental obligation. Thus, parents are under a God-mandated obligation to "preserve, nourish, and educate" their children. This is not a choice parents have. *The obligation is not to the child, but to God.* Therefore, the child may not refuse the services or release their parents from this obligation.

Fourth, parents can know and do what is best for children.

The obvious parental guide for rearing children for Locke was the Bible. Clearly, it is in the interest of the Creator in maintaining an ordered universe for a child to become a well-developed, moral adult. It is also in the interests of the child and society. Finally, it is in the best interests of the parents to bring their parental obligations to a satisfactory end and to give a good accounting of themselves to the Creator.

These were the basic Christian thought-streams that circulated through eighteenth- and nineteenth-century America. They placed basic authority in parents, but also placed obligations on parents to rear their children in what was commonly termed "the admonition of the Lord." And it was this parental authority and obligation that was embedded in the law and protected by the courts.

PART THREE

PARENTS, RIGHTS, AND THE STATE

All government originates in families, and if neglected, it will hardly exist in society. . . . The foundation of all free government and of all social order must be laid in families and in the discipline of youth.

Noah Webster
American Dictionary of the English Language (1828)
from Editor's Introduction
(reprinted 1980)

EIGHT

THE SACRED RIGHT

Recognition of the family tradition by English and American law occurs primarily in cases involving parental rights. Protection of parental rights was especially strong in the early cases.

THE COMMON LAW

The common law, which governed Western societies until the advent of modern statism, was essentially based upon Christian principles. Seton Hall University law professor John C. H. Wu writes: "Whatever you may say of its defects, which are incidental to all human institutions, there can be no denying that the common law has one advantage over the legal system of any country: it was Christian from the very beginning of its history."[1]

Essentially, the common law is an age-old doctrine that developed by way of court decisions which applied the principles of Christianity to everyday situations. Out of these cases, rules were established that governed future cases. This principle, with its origin in Europe, was carried over into the early life of America. As such, it became part of American law.

The common law is important in this discussion because it afforded a great deal of latitude to parents in dealing with their children. In fact, writes professor Bruce Hafen, the "common law recognized parental rights as a key concept [and] . . . as a fundamental cultural assumption about the family as a basic social, economic, and political unit."[2] For this reason, both English and American judges view the origins of parental rights "as being even more fundamental than property rights."[3]

Much of the children's rights literature argues that children should no longer be regarded as the "property" of their parents.[4] As the argument goes, the property mentality is still strongly embedded in Western culture. Although this may be true to some extent, the children-as-property view has not been taken seriously for many years. It was never the view of true Christianity. Moreover, the cases analyzed in this chapter, as well as the traditional limitations on the exercise of parental rights, indicate it was never really the common law view.[5]

The fact remains, however, that parental rights were ardently upheld in common law. As this has been expressed in American courts, parental rights to custody and control of minor children have been described by one American court as "sacred."[6] Another court noted that parental rights were a "natural law."[7] And yet another judge said that parental rights are "inherent, natural right[s], for the protection of which, just as much as for the protection of the rights of the individual to life, liberty, and the pursuit of happiness, our government is formed."[8]

COMMONWEALTH V. ARMSTRONG

To illustrate how strongly early American case law was in favor of parental rights, let us consider the case of *Commonwealth v. Armstrong.*[9] This Pennsylvania case was decided in 1842. It is appropriate here because it portrays how many courts in early American not only protected parental rights, but also incorporated Christian principles directly into their opinions.

The defendant, Mr. Armstrong, had refused permission and expressly prohibited the complainant, a Baptist minister, from baptizing his seventeen-year-old minor daughter (who had already been baptized in the Presbyterian church). Against the father's direct commands, and without his knowledge, the minister proceeded to baptize the girl. Upon discovering this, the father, Mr. Armstrong, was provoked to great anger and outrage. In his excitement, the father threatened the minister with personal injury. To prevent Mr. Armstrong from acting in vengeance, the court ordered him to provide surety in the sum of $500 to keep the peace for six months toward the complainant.

The court then considered the issue of who was responsible to pay the court costs involved. This issue hinged upon which party was most at fault in causing the incident. The court ruled in favor of the father. Moreover, for interfering with a father's lawful authority over his own child, the minister was ordered to pay the costs involved in the case.

Judge Lewis, speaking for the court, said:

> The authority of the father results from his duties. He is charged with the duties of *maintainance* and *education.* These cannot be performed without the authority to command and to enforce obedience. The term *education* is not limited to the ordinary instruction of the child in the pursuits of literature. It comprehends a proper attention to the *moral* and *religious sentiments* of the child. In the discharge of this duty, it is the undoubted right of the father to designate such *teachers,* either in *morals, religion* or *literature,* as *he* shall deem best calculated to give correct instruction to the child. No teacher, either in religion or in any other branch of education, has any authority over the child, *except what he derives from its parent or guardian; and that authority may be withdrawn whenever the parent, in the exercise of his discretionary power, may think proper.* . . . [H]e may prohibit such attendance and confine it to such religious teachers as he believes will be most likely to give correct instruction and to secure its welfare here, and its eternal happiness in the world to come. He cannot force it to adopt opinions contrary to the dictates of its own conscience, but he has a right to its time and its attention during its minority, for the purpose of enabling him to make the effort incumbent on him as a father, of "*training it up in the way it should go.*" . . . *The patriarchal government was established by the Most High, and,* with the necessary modification, it exists at the present day. The authority of the parent, over the youth and inexperience of his offspring, rests on foundations far more sacred than the institutions of man. "*Honor thy father and thy mother,*" was the great law proclaimed by the King of Kings. It was the first commandment accompanied with a promise of blessing upon those who obeyed it: while the dread penalty of death was inflicted upon all who were guilty of its infractions. "The eye that mocketh at his father, and despiseth to obey his mother, the ravens of the valley shall pick it out, and the young eagles shall eat it."—Proverbs 30,17. "The stubborn and rebellious son who will not obey the

voice of his father shall be stoned with stones that he may die, and all Israel shall hear and fear." Deuteronomy 21, 21. Abraham commanded his children, and his household after him, to keep the way of the Lord. Joshua *resolved both for himself and his house to serve the Lord.* And the house of Eli was destroyed because his sons made themselves vile and *he restrained* them not. "My son, keep the *instruction* of thy father and forsake not the law of thy mother." Proverbs 1, 8, 9; and Proverbs 6, 20. A fool despiseth his *father's instruction.*—Proverbs 15,5. A wise son heareth his father's instruction.—Proverbs 18,1. Cursed be he that setteth light by his father or his mother, and all the people shall say Amen.—Deuteronomy 27,16.

It was justly remarked by Horry, Professor of Moral Philosophy, in his treatise upon that subject, that the words "train up a child in the way he should go," imply both the *right* and the *duty* of the parent to train it up in the right way. That is, the way which the parent believes to be right. The right of the father to command, and the duty of the child to obey, is shown upon the authority of the Old Testament, to have been established *by God himself.* And the teachings of the New Testament abundantly prove that, instead of being abrogated in any respect, the duty of filial obedience was inculcated with all the solemn sanctions which could be derived from the New Dispensation. The fifth commandment, "Honor thy father and thy mother," was repeated and enjoined by St. Paul, in his Epistle to the Colossians. Children, obey your parents in the Lord, for this is right. Ephesians 6,1. Children, obey your parents in all things, for this is well pleasing unto the Lord. Colossians 3,20. If anything can give additional weight to the authority on which rests the doctrine of filial obedience, it is the practical commentary furnished by the Saviour himself. In his quality of GOD, it was incumbent upon him to be about business of his Heavenly Father, at Jerusalem, "both hearing the doctors, and asking them questions." But in his quality of MAN, he left the temple and its teachings of wisdom, and in obedience to the wishes of his earthly parents, "he went down with them to Nazareth, and was subject unto them." Luke iv. 51."[10]

Judge Lewis then refers to various scholars who had expounded on parental rights:

[T]he duty of children to their parents is next in order and importance to the duty we owe God. . . .

[It is] the duty of a parent to educate his children, to form them for a life of usefulness and virtue . . . and . . . he has a right to such authority, and in support of that authority to exercise such discipline as may be necessary for such purposes. . . .

[C]hildren are to regard their parents as standing in the most venerable and the most endearing of all earthly relations to them, as those to whom under God, they owe every thing they are, and every thing they hope to be. They are to regard them as the persons to whose kindness, care and *government* they have been *committed by God himself.*

"[T]he right of the parent is to command—the duty of the child is to obey. Authority belongs to the one, submission to the other. The relation . . . is established by our Creator. The failure of one party does not annilhilate the obligations of the other. If the parent be unreasonable, this does not release the child. He is still bound to honor and obey and reverence his parent."[11]

Judge Lewis then discusses the common law principles:

The doctrines of the Common law are in accordance with these principles. It is the duty of the parent to maintain and educate the child, and he possesses the resulting authority to control it in all things necessary to the accomplishment of the parent over the child, except that it must not be exercised in such a manner as to endanger its safety or morals . . . 1 Blackstone, 450; 2 Kent's Commentaries, 205. . . .

The highest judicial power in the Commonwealth dare not attempt to estrange the child from the faith of its parents. . . . Shall any man, high or low, be allowed to invade the domestic sanctuary—to disregard the parental authority established by the Almighty . . . to seduce (the child) away from its filial obedience—or even to participate in its disregard of parental authority. . . God forbid that the noblest and holiest feeling of the human heart should be thus violated—that the endearing relation of parent and child should be thus disturbed—that the harmony of the

> domestic circle should be thus broken up—and that the family altar itself should be thus rent in twain and trodden in the dust. . . . The principle of parental authority and filial obedience has its home in the human heart—is in accordance with the law of nature, and will ever be near and dear to every good man of every religion under the sun. . . . There is no limit to that authority save that which is necessary for the preservation of the health and morals of the child.[12]

As to the claim of another over the children of a particular parent, Judge Lewis notes:

> This proceeding cannot be justified under any claim founded upon the rights of conscience. The child whose *conscience* stimulates it to open rebellion against the lawful authority of its father, stands more in need of proper instruction and discipline under that authority than any other. If every child, under a claim founded upon the supposed rights of conscience, were allowed to carry into effect every decision of its immature judgment, where is that to end? Who shall prescribe limits to the crude conceptions of its youth and inexperience? Shall it be allowed, under this pretence, to violate the law of God? to repudiate the Christian religion? . . . to disregard the holy institution of marriage? . . .
>
> It is dangerous to depart from established principles. Parental authority is not to be subverted so long as it is exercised within the limits which the law has prescribed. It is the duty of the parent to REGULATE THE CONSCIENCE OF THE CHILD, by proper attention to its education; and there is no security for the offspring during the tender years of its minority but in obedience to the authority of its parents, in all things not injurious to its health or morals.[13]

Unfortunately for the Baptist minister involved, he "has transcended the divine and human law, in disregarding the authority of the father over his own offspring while in its minority. This is the opinion of the constitutional authority—the result of our conscientious convictions of the law."[14]

The eminent jurist James Kent, a giant of early American law who wrote the classic *Commentaries on American Law,* wrote to Judge Lewis commending him for his decision. Kent considered it a "just explanation and application of the parental authority" and stated his intent to put it in his *Commentaries.*[15] Moreover, the *Armstrong* case is cited as a leading authority as late as 1908.[16]

PLENARY PARENTS' RIGHTS

The rights of parents over the children under their care, as the *Armstrong* case indicates, were nearly absolute. Moreover, the early case law indicates that parental rights were established as one of the earliest forms of authority.

In fact, earlier judicial philosophy, as well as some modern judicial decision-making, imply that the parent-child relationship "antedates the state in much the same sense as natural individual rights are thought to antedate the state in American political philosophy."[17] Thus, before there was a state of any kind there were inherent human rights. Among these were those parental rights preserved within family context. Professors Philip B. Heymann and Douglas E. Barzelay write:

> *Our political system* is superimposed on and *presupposes a social system of family units,* not just of isolated individuals. *No assumption more deeply underlies our society than the assumption that it is the individual [parent] who decides whether to raise a family,* with whom to raise a family, *and,* in broad measure, *what values and beliefs to inculcate in the children who will later exercise the rights and responsibilities of citizens and heads of families. . . .*
>
> . . . *[T]he family unit does not simply co-exist with our constitutional system; it is an integral part of it.* In democratic theory as well as in practice, it is in the family that children are expected to learn the values and beliefs that democratic institutions later draw on to determine group directions. *The immensely important power of deciding about matters of early socialization has been allocated to the family, not to the government.*[18]

Parental power, the early court decisions indicate, is essentially plenary. This means it should prevail over the claims of the state, other outsiders, and the children themselves "unless there is some compelling justification for interference."[19] As a 1925 decision by the Rhode Island Supreme Court notes:

> Immemorially the family has been an important element of our civil society, one of the supports upon which our civilization has developed. Save as modified by the legislature, in domestic affairs the family has remained in law a self-governing entity under the discipline and direction of the father as its head. These fundamental principles are traceable to ancient customs and usages and are fixed by tradition and evidenced by the decisions of the courts. *Anything that brings the child into conflict with the father or diminishes the father's authority or hampers him in its exercise is repugnant to the family establishment* and is not to be countenanced save upon positive provisions of the statute law.[20]

Similarly, the Supreme Court of Mississippi, as late as 1960, has held:

> The kind and extent of education, moral and intellectual, to be given to a child and the mode of furnishing it are left largely to the discretion of the parents. . . . Unless shown to the contrary, the presumption is that natural parents will make the best decisions for their offspring. . . . [T]his important parental right is protected by common law principles. It is also a right protected by the due process clauses of the Federal and State Constitutions. . . . *The family is the basis of our society.* [The parent in the case] has an interest in [the education of his children] which lies on a different plane than that of mere property. Moreover, a child has no higher welfare than to be reared by a parent who loves him and who has not forfeited the right of custody. The agencies of our democratic government are obligated to preserve that right which is not recognized in a totalitarian society.[21]

STATE INTERFERENCE

Although parental authority has plenary overtones, it is not completely unrestricted. As such, compelling justification for state interference in parent-child relationships was recognized both at common law and in early decisions.

This is implied by the Englishman Sir William Blackstone in his *Commentaries on the Laws of England,* published between 1765 and 1770. The *Commentaries* were popular in Great Britain, but by 1775 more copies of the *Commentaries* had been sold in America than in all England.[22] Blackstone's *Commentaries,* then, were extremely influential on the development of both early American law and culture.[23] Blackstone states:

> The ancient Roman laws gave the father a power of life and death over his children; upon this principle, that he who gave had also the power of taking away. But the rigor of these laws was softened by subsequent constitutions. . . . The power of a parent, by our English laws, is much more moderate; but still sufficient to keep the child in order and obedience. He may *lawfully* correct his child, being under age, *in a reasonable manner;* for this is for the benefit of his education.[24]

A nineteenth-century English court enunciated the justifications for judicial interference in parental authority:

> A father has a legal right to control and direct the education and bringing up of his children until they attain the age of twenty-one years . . . and the Court will not interfere with him in the exercise of his paternal authority, except (1) where by his gross moral turpitude he forfeits his rights, or (2) where he has by his conduct abdicated his parental authority.[25]

It is evident that Christianity impacted English jurisprudence concerning parental rights and the early development of the law on parental rights in America. This included state interference where it was *clear* that the parents had forfeited their rights. Moreover, courts in America have increasingly expressed a "lower tolerance for serious physical harms inflicted by parents on their children."[26] This is not difficult to understand in light of the rise of child abuse in modern society.

Notwithstanding the exceptions, *parental authority in normal family situations is still vibrant.* However, as we enter the twentieth century, the older concept of the "sacred" parental rights falls into more and more question.

NINE

MERE CREATURES

A number of United States Supreme Court opinions have addressed the subject of parental prerogatives in a number of contexts. At first glance they appear to have established a strong presumption favoring parental authority. However, it must not be forgotten that the Supreme Court has not yet dealt directly with a conflict between parental rights and children's rights.

Moreover, in light of the abortion decisions from 1973 on, prior rhetoric concerning parental authority in case opinions may be tenuous. This fact, combined with weakening family structures and the children's liberation and social parenting movements, should cause concern.

But it cannot be denied that in a number of early cases the Supreme Court elevated at least a portion of the common law view of parental authority in a constitutionally guaranteed presumption favoring parental control of the family (particularly against laws calling for state intervention into the family's internal affairs). In short, these early cases established, as a constitutional right, the common law right of the parents to direct their children's upbringing.[1]

NO MERE CREATURE OF THE STATE

Two of the most significant Supreme Court rulings in this area concerned the common law right of the parents to direct the education of their children.

In *Meyer v. Nebraska*[2] the Supreme Court in 1923 established that the liberty protected by the Fourteenth Amendment due process clause included "the right of the individual to . . . establish a home and bring up children . . . and, generally, to enjoy those privileges long recognized at common law as essential to the orderly pursuit of happiness by free men."[3] The Court invalidated a state law that prohibited foreign language instruction to young school children for the reason that the law did not "promote" education, but arbitrarily and unreasonably interfered with "the natural duty of the parent to give his children education suitable to their station in life."[4]

The Court in *Meyer* rejected the state claim that patriotism and good citizenship would be advanced by ensuring that English would be the mother tongue of all children raised in the state. Acknowledging the right of German-speaking parents in an American community to have their children taught German, the Court referred expressly to the social structure discussed in Plato's *Republic.* There family life was to be replaced entirely by state child-rearing activities so pervasive that "no parent is to know his own child, nor any child his parent."[5] Commenting on such a system, the Court said:

> Although such measures have been deliberately approved by men of great genius, their ideas touching the relation between individual and State were wholly different from those upon which our institutions rest; and it hardly will be affirmed that any legislature could impose such restrictions upon the people of a State without doing violence to both letter and spirit of the Constitution.[6]

Thus, the Court in *Meyer* affirmed that the Constitution protected the cultural preferences of the parent over those of the state.

Two years later, in *Pierce v. Society of Sisters*[7] the Court struck down an Oregon compulsory education law which in effect required attendance of all children between the ages of eight and sixteen at public schools. Under the doctrine of *Meyer,* the Court said:

> The fundamental theory of liberty upon which all governments in this Union repose excludes any general power of the State to standardize its children by forcing them to

> accept instruction from public teachers only. *The child is not the mere creature of the State;* those who nurture him and direct his destiny have the right coupled with the high duty, to recognize and prepare him for additional obligations.[8]

"ITS" CHILDREN?

In 1968, in *Ginsberg v. New York*[9] the Supreme Court upheld a New York law making it illegal to sell pornographic magazines to persons under seventeen years of age. The Court identified several justifications for the restrictions, one of which was that "[c]onstitutional interpretation has consistently recognized that the parents' claim to authority in their own household to direct the rearing of their children is basic in the structure of our society."[10] More troublesome was the Supreme Court's statement in *Ginsberg* that the "state also has an independent interest in the well-being of *its* youth."[11] This appears to contradict the "mere creature" language of *Pierce v. Society of Sisters.*

In *Stanley v. Illinois*[12] the Supreme Court invalidated a state statute providing that illegitimate children, upon the death of their mother, become wards of the state without a hearing on the parental fitness of the father. In holding that the Fourteenth Amendment entitled the father to a hearing, the Court stated:

> The private interest here, that of a man in the children he has sired and raised, undeniably warrants deference and, absent a powerful countervailing interest, protection. It is plain that the interest of a parent in the companionship, care, custody, and management of his or her children come to the Court with a momentum for respect lacking when appeal is made to liberties which derive merely from shifting economic arrangements.[13]

The Court also quoted from one of its 1953 decisions which referred to parental custody rights as "[r]ights far more precious . . . than property rights."[14]

Griswold v. Connecticut,[15] which was later a cornerstone case for *Roe v. Wade,*[16] upheld the right of access of *married* persons to contraceptive information and devices. As for the family, the Court said:

> [T]he safeguarding of the home does not follow merely from the sanctity of property rights. The home derives its preeminence as the seat of family life. And the integrity of that life is something so fundamental that it has been found to draw to its protection the principles of more than one explicitly granted Constitutional right . . . The entire fabric of the Constitution and the purposes that clearly underlie its specific guarantees that *the rights to* marital privacy and to marry and *raise a family* are of similar order and magnitude as the fundamental rights specifically protected.[17]

The Supreme Court in *Griswold* specifically notes that there is a "right . . . to . . . raise a family." As such, then, this right should be constitutionally protected.

BEFORE THERE WAS A STATE

In 1972, in *Wisconsin v. Yoder*[18] the Supreme Court upheld parental claims, based on grounds of both religious freedom and parental rights, to exempt children from state compulsory education laws as applied to children beyond the eighth grade. The Court indicated that the state may not interfere with First Amendment freedoms of parents unless there is "harm to the physical or *mental health* of the child or to the public safety, peace, order, or welfare."[19] The religious freedom claim in *Yoder* was buttressed by the "history and culture of Western Civilization [which] reflect a strong tradition of parental concern for the nurture and upbringing of their children."[20]

The *Yoder* decision recognizes the *mental health exception* to parental rights. This exception would later crystallize in the trail of abortion decisions that followed *Roe v. Wade*.

A housing ordinance limiting occupancy of a dwelling unit to members of a single family (defining as a family only a few categories of related individuals, essentially parents and their children; that is, the nuclear family) was struck down by the Supreme Court in *Moore v. City of East Cleveland*.[21] This 1977 case concerned a woman who lived in her home with her son and two grandsons and was convicted of violating the ordinance because the grandsons were first cousins, not brothers.

The Supreme Court in *Moore* held that the right to live

together as a family did not extend only to the nuclear family. Justice Lewis Powell, writing for the majority, noted:

> Our is by no means a tradition limited to respect for the bonds uniting the members of the nuclear family. The tradition of uncles, aunts, cousins, and especially grandparents sharing a household along with parents and children has roots equally venerable and equally deserving of constitutional recognition.[22]

Powell further noted:

> Our decisions establish that *the Constitution protects the sanctity of the family* precisely because the institution of the family is deeply rooted in this nation's history and tradition. It is through the family that we inculcate and pass down many of our cherished values, moral and cultural.[23]

In the same year that *Moore* was decided, the Supreme Court handed down its decision in *Smith v. Organization of Foster Families for Equality and Reform.*[24] In this case the Court addressed the constitutional standards for the removal of foster children from the care of foster parents. The Court found New York's removal procedures adequate to satisfy whatever interests the foster parents may have.

Implicitly recognizing that the extent of psychological commitment in a foster-care relationship could be significant, the Court in *Smith* still found that the nature of the foster parents' constitutional interest did not rise to the level of natural parents' interests. The Court specifically pointed out that recognition of rights in the foster parents could affect the rights of the child's natural parents.[25]

The Court, however, in *Smith* made an important distinction. It noted that the foster parents' interest originates in a state contract.[26] The interests of the natural parents, on the other hand, originate in "intrinsic human rights" that are antecedent to the state.[27]

In other words, before there was a state, there were parents already in existence. Thus, by implication parental rights are foundational to all other rights.

TERMINATION

There has been a concerted effort in many states to terminate parental rights for neglect, cruelty, or the like. The Court addressed this issue in 1982 in *Santosky v. Kramer.*[28]

In *Santosky* the Court held that states may not terminate parental rights based on the evidentiary standard of a preponderance of the evidence, but must support its allegations by at least "clear and convincing evidence."[29] The Court pointed to the grave threat of erroneous termination, noting that "few forms of state action are both so severe and so irreversible."[30] The Court explained:

> When the State initiates a parental rights termination proceeding, it seeks not merely to infringe that fundamental liberty interest, but to end it. "If the State prevails it will have worked a unique kind of deprivation . . . A parent's interest in the accuracy and justice of the decision to terminate his or her parental status is, therefore, a commanding one." . . . Few forms of state action are both so severe and so irreversible.[31]

The Court even noted that the state's interest should be in preserving the parent-child relationship wherever possible:

> Yet while there is still reason to believe that positive, nurturing parent-child relationships exist, the [state's] . . . interest favors preservation, not severance, of natural familial bonds. "The State registers no gain towards its declared goals when it separates children from the custody of fit parents."[32]

The *Santosky* decision reiterated the idea that termination must be based on a substantial showing of unfitness, and the state at every phase must provide the parents with fundamentally fair procedures.[33] As the opinion expressed it:

> *The fundamental liberty interest of natural parents in the care, custody, and management of their child does not evaporate simply because they have not been model parents or have lost temporary custody to the State.* Even when blood

> relationships are strained, parents retain a vital interest in preventing the irretrievable destruction of their family life. If anything, persons faced with forced dissolution of their parental rights have a more critical need for procedural protections than do those resisting state intervention into ongoing family affairs. When the State moves to destroy weakened familial bonds, it must provide the parents with fundamentally fair procedures.[34]

WHY IS IT IMPORTANT?

In spite of the Supreme Court's apparent agreement on the general notion that parents have rights, the cases really shed no true light on why parental rights should be recognized. The older cases specifically noted that they were relying on Christian principles. However, the modern phobia over the separation of church and state prevents *any* reference to the Christian principles in terms of them being truth. However, "the language chosen by many judges who have dealt with parental interest issues," writes professor Bruce Hafen, "suggests that more is at stake than the welfare of children."[35]

The Supreme Court in *Meyer v. Nebraska* concluded that parents have the rights "to establish a home and bring up children."[36] In *Stanley v. Illinois* the Court recognized "the interest of a parent in the companionship, care, custody, and management of his or her children."[37] Also, as Hafen says:

> The right of parents to bring suits against third parties for alienation of the affections of their children has been recognized within the limited categories of relational interests protected by common law tort actions. Parents may also recover for injuries to that relational interest under most wrongful death statutes, just as children may recover under those statutes for the death of a parent.[38]

These decisions may be due to both the psychological and cultural recognition of *the uniqueness of intrafamily relationships*. A 1974 federal appeals court decision acknowledges interests of this kind. The court recognized the standing of a father to bring a civil rights action against police officers who had shot and killed his son.[39] The court said: "The familial relationship between parent and child is fundamental to our civilization," and "[t]he practical effect of [the shooting by the policeman] was to deny the plaintiff [the father] *the fundamental right to raise his son.*"[40]

But why is it a fundamental right? Parroting this sentiment in a string of decisions does not answer the question of why we cherish the parent-child relationship.

It may be best explained in terms of the cultural memory of that relationship that existed in the past—a time when the Christian idea that children are gifts from God was an assumed principle. And parents, in reflecting the Creator's concern and care for all His creatures, earnestly sought to care for, nurture, and protect their children.

ILLUSIONS

The Supreme Court has made important statements that seem to uphold parental authority. However, glimpses of the Court's underlying foundation appear when the Court refers to "its" children or creates "mental health" exceptions.

Clearly, if the state has an arguable interest in children as creatures of the state and can remove or penalize parents for alleged mental health harm to children, then the so-called "sacred" rights of parents are illusory. And when and if the statist hammer falls, cultural memories will not afford any true protection.

TEN

THE PARENT STATE

Since the civil rights movement of the 1950s and 1960s and recent Supreme Court decisions giving constitutional dimensions to certain rights for children, new questions concerning parental authority have been raised. The civil rights movement and activism of the 1960s raised the social conscience of a large number of people.

As a result, many of the same people (including students) who became involved in the civil rights movement were later attracted to other causes. Besides the women's rights movement (which later developed into an extreme feminism for some) and the other causes, focus was turned toward the rights of children. This, of course, was heightened by the increasing horror stories surrounding child abuse.

However, we must not see extreme feminism and the children's liberation movement as separate. They are simply one stream that seeks to break with tradition. In their radical stages, they advocate an irresponsibility that seeks autonomous rights, no matter the cost.

For these movements to succeed, they would need to be constitutionally protected. They found legal justification in two areas that significantly impact on the rights of parents. The first is students' rights; the second is the right to sexual freedom and abortion as a constitutional right.

A SUBSTITUTE FAMILY

Ironically, all the twentieth-century movements for rights or freedom from restraint have coincided with the rise of statism.

> time. On the subsequent votes ask the students to vote as they feel their parents would vote, then as their grandparents might vote. Discuss reasons for differences.[15]

One parent from Oregon testified concerning a guidance and counseling curriculum used in their local public school. Her son was given "decision" questionnaires:

> We all make decisions daily. Some are more important than others. Some require thought and study before making, and others are almost made automatically. The following decisions are faced by many people today. Read them and decide which decision category applies to each. Write the number code in the blank after the decisions to tell how much thought you put into each one.
>
> 0—Not under my control
> 1—Automatic—no thought
> 2—Sometimes think about it
> 3—Think about, but do not study
> 4—Study a little bit
> 5—Study a lot.
>
> *Typical Decisions*
>
> 1. To get up in the morning.
> 2. What to eat and when
> 3. To tell the truth
> 4. To criticize a friend behind his back
> 5. To drink alcohol
> 6. To work a job
> 7. To use drugs besides alcohol
> 8. To smoke
> 9. To follow school rules
> 10. To vandalize
> 11. To go to school
> 12. To lie to your parents
> 13. To believe in God
> 14. Where to dispose of paper and wrappers
> 15. What movie to see.[16]

Some very private questions concerning parents were asked:

The invasions of privacy in this curriculum are endless.

> Do you have your own bedroom?
>
> Are you going to practice religion just like your parents?
>
> Who has the last word in your family?
>
> Draw a picture of your house and family occupants; write what each one is saying.
>
> Draw what your parents wear at home, at work.
>
> What tools do they use at home, at work?
>
> What is your parents' income?
>
> How much time do your parents spend watching TV?[17]

These are not merely isolated instances. This type of activity is occurring nationwide. These are matters traditionally left solely to parents. It represents an attempt—again, whether it is intentional or not is inconsequential—by the state school system to become "the" parent of all children. And it represents a radical departure from the past.

However, it is to be expected. If the state has the authority to compel children to attend school and to establish public schools, then it logically follows that the state has *a* claim to children. The state is then, in some context, a parent. This means that the child has an existence, again in some context, independent from the parent in the public school. Tragically, the Supreme Court has recognized this fact.

PARENS PATRIAE

The state's historical claim to any authority over children is found in the doctrine of *parens patriae*. This is a Latin phrase which essentially means that the state is the parent.

It has been adopted in this country from English law. In Great Britain, it is used to justify the state's assumption of a protective parental role in certain situations, including those where the traditional parental role breaks down.

In America, court decisions as early as 1839 were referring to the doctrine as appropriate in cases of delinquent or neglected children.[18] As one court said: "The right of parental control is a natural, but not an unalienable one."[19]

Much of the impetus for the development of the *parens patriae* doctrine came with the plight of children from the midnineteenth century onward. As America began to develop and urbanization increased, children became less and less an asset and more of a liability. Homeless children became a reality in the large cities. And with the coming of industrialization, children were placed on the assembly line.

The Industrial Revolution intensified the call for more state care of children. Urbanization and industrialization of society during the eighteenth and nineteenth centuries led to the cruel exploitation of children in factories and mills. Many worked like slaves; some worked sixteen hours per day.

It was during this era that momentum began building for state protection of children. This brought with it a wave of reformers who called for measures to protect children and, if necessary, intervene in family affairs. The reformers were, in essence, attempting to recapture or rediscover the earlier concept of childhood that was waning before an age of mechanization.

By the midnineteenth century, laws were passed authorizing courts to commit neglected, destitute, abandoned, and vagrant children to "Houses of Refuge," "juvenile asylums," reform schools, and other institutions. Most of these were established by *private* corporations that receive public funds. These early efforts were more preventive than protective, since they were aimed at preventing neglected children from entering a life of crime and threatening the state.

In the latter part of the nineteenth century, cruelty societies—which, amazingly enough, had first been formed to protect animals—began to concern themselves with the protection of children as well. In a famous case in 1874, an attorney for the American Society for the Prevention of Cruelty to Animals, upon the request of a social worker, intervened on behalf of the abused child. Later, "Societies for the Prevention of Cruelty to Children" (SPCC) were organized in every major city.[20]

Originally the reformers took a "law enforcement" approach, seeing to it that laws concerning children were strictly enforced. Gradually the concern shifted to preventive, remedial and economic efforts that would strengthen the home so that the child might remain with his parents. However, in most instances, "law enforcement" efforts would mean state intervention.

The broadly worded and vague statutes which gave the state

the right to intervene into the family were generally upheld during the nineteenth century under the doctrine of *parens patriae*. The *parens patriae* doctrine received a boost in 1899 with the establishment of the first juvenile court in Chicago. A law was also passed in 1899 in Illinois which incorporated the concept of *parens patriae* by providing that "the care, custody and discipline of a child shall approximate as nearly as may be that which should be given by its parents."[21] The law also gave certain individual and social agencies "parental" rights. This included the right to place the child in a family home and to consent to the child's adoption without notice to or consent from the child's natural parents.[22]

As these types of laws spread across the country, the state began to assume a more general authority over children. In fact, as professor Mason Thomas notes, the general thrust of such laws was to displace parents who were viewed as failures and to substitute the state as the parent.[23] By 1920, however, all but three states had a juvenile court system.

Neglect proceedings were generally within the jurisdiction of the juvenile courts, and in interpreting the broadly worded statutes the courts sometimes looked beyond the express language to incorporate the standard used in civil custody disputes—"the best interests of the child." Thus, the emphasis in family disputes began to shift away from the authority of parents to the "rights" of children.

In custody rights cases today, most courts will base the custody decision on "the best interests of the child" (although many states cling to the traditional rule that a parent is entitled to custody unless proven unfit). Moreover, many states have recently passed laws allowing courts to permanently terminate parental rights in cases of "extreme" neglect or abuse.

Soon to follow were mandatory reporting laws which were proposed in the early 1960s. Between 1963 and 1967 all fifty states had enacted some version of the reporting laws (forty-four mandatory, and six voluntary). Under the mandatory reporting laws, physicians are required to report cases to police authorities when they have reasonable cause to believe that a child has suffered serious physical injury by other than accidental means from a parent or caretaker. Other versions require the physician to report the suspected abuse to child welfare agencies.[24]

Finally, with the activism of the 1960s and the involvement of the courts and legislatures in student and children's issues, it was evident that society was shifting toward more concern for children and their rights. As parents chafed at the new definitions of rights and liberties, conflicts in the coming years were a certainty.

A basic concept involved in the *parens patriae* philosophy is that children can, after a certain determination, be made *wards* of the state—even if they have natural parents. The same mentality can be, with some modifications, carried over to other public institutions (such as the public schools). With the rise of the children's liberation movement, maybe it was inevitable.

THE STATE AS PARENT

Within the last several decades, the Supreme Court has begun addressing children's rights in constitutional terms.

For example, in the case of *In re Gault*[25] in 1967, the Court established the principle that minor children may not be denied basic rights in juvenile court proceedings. Justice Abe Fortas wrote that "neither the Fourteenth Amendment nor the Bill of Rights is for adults alone."[26]

A major area in which the Supreme Court has acknowledged children's rights in constitutional dimensions is the public school setting. In *Tinker v. Des Moines Independent School District,*[27] the Court found that the First Amendment rights of three students had been violated when school authorities suspended them from school for wearing black armbands to protest the government's policy in Vietnam. Writing for the Court, Justice Fortas stated that, "[s]tudents in school as well as out of school are 'persons' under the Constitution. They are possessed of fundamental rights which the State must respect."[28]

Several of the justices were concerned with what seemed to be a sweeping decision. Potter Stewart, for example, said he could not "share the Court's uncritical assumption that, school discipline aside, the First Amendment rights of children are co-extensive with those of adults."[29]

The implications of the *Tinker* decision are obvious. The public schools, which are to stand *in loco parentis* to their students, are, to some degree, now a public forum for free speech activities.

If the *Tinker* rationale is transferred to the family unit, another implication is clear: the right to resist school authorities is, in essence, the right to resist parental authority. Similarly, is the family a free speech forum for all family members, including children? Justice Hugo Black in his dissent in *Tinker* expressed great concern over the implications of the decision:

> [I]f the time has come when pupils of state-supported schools, kindergartens, grammar schools, or high schools can defy and flout orders of school officials to keep their minds on their own schoolwork, it is the beginning of a new revolutionary era of permissiveness in this country fostered by the judiciary. The next logical step, it appears to me, would be to hold unconstitutional laws that bar pupils under 21 and 18 from voting or from being elected members of the boards of education . . . The original idea of schools, which I do not believe is yet abandoned as worthless or not out of date, was that children had not yet reached the point of experience and wisdom which enabled them to teach all of their elders.[30]

Six years later Justice Lewis Powell expressed a similar concern in his dissent in *Goss v. Lopez.*[31] In *Goss* the Supreme Court held that students facing temporary disciplinary suspensions from a public school are entitled to such due process protections as prior notice and an opportunity for a hearing.[32] Powell said:

> [T]he Court ignores the experience of mankind as well as the long history of our law, recognizing that there are differences which must be accommodated in determining the rights and duties of children as compared with those of adults. Examples of this distinction abound in our law: in contracts, in torts, in criminal law and procedure, in criminal sanctions and rehabilitation, and in the right to vote and to hold office. Until today, and except in the special context of the First Amendment issue in *Tinker,* the educational rights of children and teenagers in the elementary and secondary schools have not been analogized to the rights of adults or to those accorded college students. Even with respect to the First Amendment, the rights of children have not been regarded as "co-existensive with those of adults."[33]

Both the constitutional and cultural tensions are obvious. Who is the real parent? Do the public schools really stand in place of the parents?

The Supreme Court in a 1985 decision took a giant stride in establishing parental claims in the state. In *New Jersey v. T.L.O.*[34] the Court restricted the authority of public school officials to search students. The Court, speaking through Justice White, said:

> Teachers and school administrators, it is said, act *in loco parentis* in their dealing with students: Their authority is that of the parent, not the State. . . . Such reasoning is in tension with contemporary reality and the teachings of this Court. . . . If *school authorities are state actors* for purposes of the constitutional guarantees of freedom of expression and due process, it is difficult to understand why they should be deemed to be exercising parental rather than public authority when conducting searches of their students. More generally, the Court has recognized that "the concept of parental delegation" as a source of school authority is not entirely "consonant with compulsory education laws." . . . *Today's public school officials do not merely exercise authority voluntarily conferred on them by individual parents; rather, they act in furtherance of publicly mandated educational and disciplinary policies. . . . [S]chool officials act as representatives of the State, not merely as surrogates for the parents . . .*[35]

CONFLICT

Therefore, in terms of public education, the Supreme Court has, in the last twenty years, promoted at least two basic themes. First, children do have rights *independent* of their parents. Second, the public school no longer represents the parent, but is an *independent* institution that represents the interests of the state.

It logically follows, then, that when children are under the authority of public school officials, they are not under the authority of their parents. The shift has been subtle, but it lays the groundwork for some intense conflicts between parents on one side and the child and state on the other.

ELEVEN

KILLING THE FAMILY

In the early history of this country, the courts, especially the United States Supreme Court, upheld traditional family autonomy. These early cases rested upon a Christian understanding of the marriage relationship. The United States Supreme Court's 1888 opinion in *Maynard v. Hill*[1] is illustrative of this long line of precedent:

> [W]hilst marriage is often termed by text writers and in decisions of courts a civil contract . . . it is something more than a mere contract. The consent of the parties is of course essential to its existence, but when the contract to marry is executed by the marriage, a relation between the parties is created which they cannot change. Other contracts may be modified, restricted, or enlarged, or entirely released upon the consent of the parties. Not so with marriage. The relation once formed, the law steps in and holds the parties to various obligations and liabilities. It is an institution, the maintenance of which in its purity the public is deeply interested, for it is the foundation of the family and of society, without which there would be neither civilization nor progress.[2]

Given this view of marriage as a "status" or "institution" and not merely as a "contract," the various functions assigned to the family were protected from state encroachment. Thus, the Court from *Meyer v. Nebraska*[3] to *Moore v. East Cleveland*[4] could lay down rules of law that favored parental control over their children and that favored familial choices in living arrangements.

Even the question of the proper use of contraceptives was considered by the Supreme Court in *Griswold v. Connecticut*[5] to belong to the family on the assumption that the appropriate authority over the intimate sexual life of the husband and wife was lodged in the family unit, not the state. However, beginning in the early 1970s, the Supreme Court launched a new line of cases that marked a sharp break from the past.

THE RIGHT TO CHOOSE

In 1972 in *Eisenstadt v. Baird*,[6] the Supreme Court extended the right to determine the appropriate use of contraceptives to *unmarried* persons. The significance of this decision to the Court's later decisions that have actively fostered the breakdown of the family unit has been recognized by at least one legal scholar:

> The rationale in *Griswold* was at least logical and historical, even if unarticulated in the Constitution; and, historically the Court had upheld the marital institution in glowing terms which followed the traditional Christian explanation. But *Eisenstadt* completely failed the traditional test since no such right had ever been found in the "rooted traditions" of the American people. . . . *Eisenstadt* . . . represents a radical departure with little or no constitutional foundation or development either in American legal history or in case law.[7]

The logic of *Eisenstadt* flows inexorably into the abortion decision of *Roe v. Wade*.[8] "The right to abortion was founded on the right to privacy which was said to be located in the ninth or fourteenth amendments," writes attorney Peter Riga. "But more importantly, no distinction was made between the unmarried plaintiff, Jane Roe, and the married plaintiff, Mary Doe."[9]

Underlying these decisions, as defined through the right to privacy, was the idea that people have a *right to choose* certain lifestyles or modes of expression even in the context of the family. Thus, the "choice" of the individual takes preference even if exercised within the family and even if it is detrimental to the stability of the traditional family unit.

ROE V. WADE

In 1973 in *Roe v. Wade,* the Supreme Court elevated, in the name of a so-called constitutional "right" of privacy, a woman's right to "mental health" above the life of an unborn child in her womb. In *Roe* Justice Harry Blackmun admitted that the "Constitution does not explicitly mention any right to privacy."[10] Nevertheless, Blackmun went on to "create" the right in terms of abortion (supposedly relying on earlier Supreme Court precedent).[11]

In at least the first six months of pregnancy, the woman was granted a constitutional right to abortion if upon consultation with her physician it was decided that her health would be jeopardized by having the baby. Blackmun wrote:

> Maternity, or additional offspring, may force upon the woman a *distressful* life and future. *Psychological harm* may be imminent. *Mental and physical health* may be taxed by child care. There is also the distress, for all concerned, associated with the unwanted child, and there is the problem of bringing a child into a family already unable, *psychologically* and otherwise, to care for it. In other cases, as in this one, the additional difficulties and *continuing stigma* of unwed motherhood may be involved. All these are factors the woman and her responsible physician necessarily will consider in consultation.[12]

The life of the unborn child was thus subordinated to the woman's *convenience*—that is, stress and psychological or mental stress is enough to justify killing children. The Court, in essence, approved abortion-on-demand.[13]

KILLING CHILDREN

In *Planned Parenthood v. Danforth*[14] the Supreme Court ruled unconstitutional a Missouri statute that required the husband's consent before a married woman's decision to abort a child. The statute obviously reinforced the traditional patriarchal design of the family. However, the Court ruled that the state could not constitutionally reinforce that family structure to the detriment of the wife's right of choice.

In a remarkable argument, in which Justice Blackmun disregards both the family's existence independent of the power of the state and the husband's interest in the unborn child as a party in the impregnation process, the Court dismissed the Missouri statute as follows:

> Clearly, since the State cannot regulate or proscribe abortion during the first stage . . . the State cannot delegate authority to any particular person, even the spouse, to prevent abortion during that same period. . . .
>
> The obvious fact is that when the wife and the husband disagree on the decision, the view of only one of the two marriage partners can prevail. Since it is the woman who physically bears the child and who is the more directly and immediately affected by the pregnancy, as between the two, the balance weighs in her favor.[15]

Blackmun argued that the Missouri consent law did *not* foster marital relationships. He said:

> [W]e recognize that the decision to undergo or forgo an abortion may have profound effects on the future of any marriage, effects that are both *physical and mental*, and possibly deleterious. Notwithstanding these factors, we cannot hold that the State has the constitutional authority to give the spouse unilaterally the ability to prohibit the wife from terminating her pregnancy, when the State itself lacks the right.[16]

The other members of the family, then, are subordinated to the convenience of the pregnant woman.

In the *Danforth* case, the Court also ruled unconstitutional a Missouri statute which required written consent of a parent or guardian of an *unmarried* woman under the age of eighteen to obtain an abortion during the first trimester of pregnancy. Again the Court endorsed a constitutional principle diametrically opposed to traditional family autonomy.

The United States District Court had previously upheld the parental consent provision. The district court found "a compelling basis . . . in the State's interest 'in safeguarding the authority of the family relationship.' "[17]

Justice Blackmun disagreed with this proposition and noted that such a consent provision, in his opinion, did not safeguard the family unit or enhance parental authority.[18] He stated: "Any independent interest the parent may have in the termination of the minor daughter's pregnancy is no more weighty than the right of privacy of the competent minor mature enough to have become pregnant."[19] *The interest of the parents to control the upbringing of their minor daughter was thus subordinated to their daughter's convenience.*

In terms of abortion, then, the Court has fostered the autonomous wife and the autonomous child. Not only is this detrimental to the traditional family structure, but it is also injurious to women and children.

Our atomistic culture is devouring women and children. Children are aborted, and in many instances if a child survives the abortion, he or she is left to die on the operating table. If the child survives into childhood, the chances that the child will be physically abused are high.

The total effects of the women's liberation movement have yet to be fully evaluated. One certain effect has been the redefining of the woman's role in the home as well as her relationship to her husband and her children (if any).

Instead of being the cradle of future generations, modern women, in large part, have been reduced to sexual parity with men. The concept that women belong to a higher estate than men has waned in recent years. George Gilder writes: "They must relinquish their sexual superiority, psychologically disconnect their wombs, and adopt the short circuited copulatory sexuality of males."[20]

Women, once the center of the home, are now, in many instances, the receptacles of male sexual frustrations. And now, if pregnancy does result from sexual union, the abortion avenue is open. Essentially, *abortion legalizes murder in the life of the family at the choice of the "mother."* Indeed, the cradle of life has become the cradle of death.

As the traditional family fades, the vacuum it leaves is being filled with "a bewildering array of family forms: homosexual marriages, communes, groups of elderly people banding together to share expenses (and sometimes sex), tribal grouping among certain ethnic minorities, and many other forms coexist as never before."[21] In fact, recent statistics indicate that one-parent "families" now account for 26 percent of all "families" with children.[22]

The implications of the abortion decisions are ominous for the family in other areas. Already the Court has extended the principle of child autonomy beyond abortion.

For example, in *Carey v. Population Services International*,[23] the Court held that a state statute which restricts the sale of contraceptives to those over sixteen years of age, and then only by a licensed pharmacist, is contrary to the right of privacy of minors. It is therefore unconstitutional.

In response to this newly declared right, one federal court of appeals has held that minors possess a right of privacy which includes the right to obtain contraceptives without having to consult their parents. Although acknowledging that parents are interested in contraceptives being distributed to their children, the court held there is no duty on the part of a family planning center to notify the parents concerned.[24]

In *H. L. v. Matheson*,[25] the Supreme Court did uphold the constitutionality of a Utah statute which requires a physician to "notify, if possible" the parents of a dependent, unmarried minor girl prior to performing an abortion. This decision appears to *reduce parents to the level of state-employed consultants.*

CREATING THE CONFLICT

The parallel between the public school cases—such as *Tinker* and *Goss*—and the *Danforth* case, wherein the Supreme Court made it clear that the state has no constitutional authority to grant the parents veto authority over their minor daughter's decision to obtain an abortion, is a remarkable one. In *Danforth*, the Court declared that "[c]onstitutional rights do not mature and come into being magically only when one attains the state-defining age of majority. Minors, as well as adults, are protected by the Constitution and possess constitutional rights."[26]

However, the *Danforth* case, if carried to its logical conclusion of extending fundamental rights to children, carries serious implications. As professor Bruce Hafen writes:

> [T]he uncritical application of egalitarian theory to children places them and their parents on the same plane in their relationship to the state. This apparently subtle shift has the enormous effect of removing parents from a "line position" between the state and their children, which not only exposes families to the risks of direct state access to children, but which raises basic new questions about the nature of parental responsibility. . . . For one thing, *the state could revoke or limit its delegation, and in no case could "parents" exercise greater authority than could the state.*[27]

There is yet another disturbing implication of Justice Blackmun's opinion in *Danforth*. That is: the Court's "view reflects a surprising insensitivity to the distinction between public and private action generally and to the private authority of parents in particular. It also seems to assume that state support for parental authority falls automatically into the category of 'state action' for Fourteenth Amendment purposes."[28]

In speaking of the "right to personal autonomy. . . autonomy which is particularly important for young people in their developmental stage,"[29] one writer states: "The first amendment is premised on a belief that regimentation of mind and spirit block the advancement of knowledge and the discovery of truth; state regulation or state-sanctioned parental interference that intrudes on areas of belief and puts undue restrictions on spiritual development is inimical to these important developmental values."[30]

To some, then, any state sanction of parental control over children translates into state action. Therefore, in such instances *the child's constitutional rights and state enforcement of those rights come into play:*

> [C]hildren will have to continue to rely on state protection of their religious interests as against their parents, and of course any state efforts to vindicate their interests are limited by parental constitutional rights recognized in *Pierce* and *Yoder.* A case could arise if the state did seek to protect the religious rights of minors. This conflict would be between the child's state-supported interest in religious freedom (not the child's constitutional right) and the parents' constitutionally protected rights.[31]

Finally, *troublesome* is the view of marriage expressed in *Danforth* by the Supreme Court. Traditional marriage was a covenanted community formed from the consent of both parties. Therefore, it was something more profound than the individuals who composed it.

On the other hand, the Court's view of marriage in *Danforth* follows the reasoning of the *Eisenstadt* decision. In *Eisenstadt,* marriage is seen as a tenuous union formed by the consensual agreement of the two individuals who remain autonomous and independent throughout the relationship. As Peter Riga comments:

> Since this is so, then the decision to abort comes down on the autonomous individual who has the most to lose, gain, suffer, etc., in a sort of balancing process of advantages versus disadvantages. In this instance the woman does the balancing. No heed is given to the unbreakable unity or covenant, where the marital institution is greater than its composite individuals, because this no longer exists as a definition of marriage.[32]

IN LOCO CAESAR

Have the courts abandoned *Meyer v. Nebraska,* in which it was presupposed that the child was not the mere creature of the state? The recent decisions of the Supreme Court seem to indicate that the family is no longer the basic institution for determining values for children. Instead, that is the state's province in and through its various agencies.

In *Wisconsin v. Yoder* Justice William O. Douglas in his dissent remarked:

> If the parents in this case are allowed a religious exception, the inevitable effect is to impose the parents' notions of religious duty upon their children. Where the child is mature enough to express potentially conflicting desires, *it would be an invasion of the child's rights to permit such an imposition without canvassing his views.* . . . As the child has no other effective forum, it is in this litigation that his rights should be considered. And, if an Amish child desires to attend high school, and is *mature* enough to have that

> desire respected, *the State may well be able to override the parents' religiously motivated objections.*[33]

In reply to Douglas' dissent in upholding the right of the Amish to withhold their children from school, the majority of justices stated:

> The dissent argues that a child who expresses a desire to attend public high school in conflict with the wishes of the parents should not be prevented from doing so. There is no reason for the Court to consider that point since it is not an issue in the case.[34]

Therefore, the Supreme Court has left a question mark concerning whether or not a child has a constitutional right to refuse direction and, in particular, instruction—religious or otherwise—from his parents based upon the "maturity" factor.

But how is maturity to be defined? The Supreme Court has set no precise standard. Indeed, in *H. L. v. Matheson* the Court declined to define that term even though crucial to the case. Is the appraisal of maturity to be left to the social engineers? The problem is that the social engineers disagree.

Some courts have already recognized that adolescent children are sufficiently mature to exercise meaningfully the right to choose among competing religious beliefs. This is reflected in a number of custody dispute cases where children have been allowed to make their own choice on the issue of religion. For example, in *Hehman v. Hehman*[35] a New York court ordered that a dispute between parents as to a child's religious upbringing be referred to an official referee, who would interview the thirteen-year-old boy involved to determine his own religious preference. The court noted the boy's age and the fact that he had been exposed to both his parents' creeds.[36] The *Hehman* court concluded that the decision should be left to the child, who could not "be forced to enter a religion against his wishes."[37]

Harvard law professor Laurence Tribe argues that when the parents "threaten the autonomous growth and expression of [family] members [read: children] . . . then there is no longer any reason to protect family authority."[38] Who, however, is going to exercise the authority to determine when children are threatened by the family? The state, of course. *In loco parentis* has become *in loco Caesar.*

HELPING THE DEMISE

From the beginning to the present, the Supreme Court has echoed sentiments that tend toward supporting traditional family autonomy in the conduct of internal affairs. Even in *Danforth* Justice Blackman noted: "Parental discretion . . . has been protected from unwarranted or unreasonable interference from the State."[39] Likewise, in another Supreme Court case, in striking down a parental consent law for abortion, Justice Powell stated:

> While we do not pretend any special wisdom on this subject, we cannot ignore that central to many of these theories, and deeply rooted in our Nation's history and tradition, is the belief that the parental role implies a substantial measure of authority over one's children. Indeed, "constitutional interpretation has consistently recognized that the parents' claim to authority in their own household to direct the rearing of their children is basic in the structure of our society."[40]

And in *H. L. v. Matheson* we find Justice Warren Burger saying:

> We have recognized on numerous occasions that the relationship between parent and child is constitutionally protected. See, e.g., *Wisconsin v. Yoder . . . Stanley v. Illinois . . . Meyer v. Nebraska . . .* "It is cardinal with us that the custody, care and nurture of the child reside first in the parents, whose primary function and freedom include preparation for obligations the state can neither supply nor hinder."[41]

On one hand the Court has been trumpeting the virtues of family autonomy and parental authority, while on the other it has been rendering decisions which strike at the heart of family authority. The family is in trouble, and the Supreme Court and our culture seem to be furthering its demise. If only they would heed the advice of Supreme Court Justice William Rehnquist:

> Surely the family must be at the top of the list of these institutions or infrastructures and, so long as it is a going concern, must be treated very gingerly by the law, avoiding any intrusion into the traditional family decision-making process. It is not a question of developing rules of law deferential to the family; it is the need to recognize that there should rarely be judicial intervention at *all* in families which are "going concerns." Damage results merely by allowing resort to the legal process, no matter what the outcome on the merits may be. The law would be well-advised to recognize the limits of its competence and decline to allow family members resort to the courts when they are dissatisfied with the decision of the family. If the day ever arrives when special counsel must be appointed for a six-year-old whose parents, following the advice of their physician have decided the child must have a tonsillectomy, we will have permitted the adversary process familiar to business disputes and differing views of public law to overwhelm an already fragile institution.[42]

PART FOUR

CHILDREN, RIGHTS, AND HUMANITY

Sing a song of students' rights,
An issue full of woe;
First and Fourteenth Amendment rights
Violated long ago.
Remember, in the good old days,
That old Jack Seaver case;
The courts said we had every right
To keep 'em in their place!

Students had few rights
That schools needed to respect;
So we socked it to them
By bushel and by peck.

We made them pledge, we made them salute,
We even had them pray;
We got support from the court
And from the PTA!

From Gobitis *through* Pugsley
We really poured it on;
And when they didn't do our thing,
Suspended! They were gone.
But then there came the Iowa case,
I believe we called it "Tinker";
The courts reversed the things they'd done,
And that became a stinker!

Now, we celebrate
Our Bi-cen-ten-ni-al;
With Wood-Strickland, *and* Goss-Lopez,
Alas, it's pe-ren-ni-al.
There's no teaching; There's no learning;
What are we to do?
I guess there's only one solution;
It's our turn to sue!

Robert L. Mc Ginnis
Sing a Song of Students' Rights (1976)

TWELVE

THE RIGHTS OF CHILDREN

It cannot be denied that *children do have rights*. The antiabortion movement is premised on the fact that unborn children have, at the minimum, the right to life.

The question involved is, then, not whether children have rights; it concerns what rights they possess. Also, what limits are or should be placed on the rights of children.

PROTECTION VERSUS CHOICE

Emerging from the train of history, there are those who argue for absolute equality of children and adults. These liberationists ignore the fact that when children are involved, a significant distinction must be made. It is between the *rights of protection* and *the rights of choice*.

The *rights of protection* are rights that protect one from undue interference by the state. They also protect one from harmful acts of others.[1]

The rights of protection include the right not to be imprisoned without due process of law, rights of property, and rights to physical protection. "The protection category," Bruce Hafen notes, "seems to embrace most, if not all, of the legal doctrines that have developed to date for the benefit of minors in both the constitutional context and juvenile law context."[2]

Laws creating juvenile court jurisdiction, despite the *parens patriae* implications, are also in the protection category. They are ostensibly designed to protect children against harmful abuse, neglect, or abandonment by their natural parents or others.

Moreover, the entire juvenile justice system is based upon the premise that children are yet in the developmental stages of becoming mature adults. As such, they "should be protected against the long-term implications of their own decisions made at a time when they lack sufficient capacity and experience to be held as responsible as an adult would be for the same decision."[3]

In all legal inquiries involving children, traditionally it has been assumed that minors do not have the same basic capacities as adults. This has been preeminent in cases involving juveniles.

Children develop from incapacity to capacity. The question is where to draw the age line above which a given right or activity may be permitted. Again, such a consideration assumes that the children do not have capacity but develop it.

However, to "presume, to the contrary, that rational judgmental capacities exist until evidence demonstrates otherwise is to defy both logic and experience, *because the evidence already demonstrates from the outset that capacities among infants are negligible.*"[4] Thus, the presumption of incapacity to make certain choices is compelled by nature.

The *rights of choice* are legal rights that permit persons to make affirmative choices of binding consequence. This includes such rights as voting, marrying, exercising religious preference, and choosing whether to seek education.

The presumptions arising from the limited capacities of children account, in large part, for their general limitation on the exercise of "choice" rights. The law, and traditionally the culture, has assumed that a basic capacity to make responsible choices is a prerequisite to meaningful exercise of such rights.

An example is the age limitation on voting rights. As the United States Supreme Court recognized in 1970, the age limitation on voting rights has been thought to fix the level above which citizens "are capable of intelligent and responsible exercise of the right to vote."[5] This restriction has prevailed even though the right to vote is one of the most fundamental citizenship rights.

Presumably, also for general reasons of capacity, the United States Constitution expressly limits membership in the House of Representatives and the Senate on the basis of age (and lists age as a qualification for the Presidency).[6] There are other examples of age limitations as well:

> Other illustrations abound, from statutes fixing the age below which one may not marry without parental consent to long-standing common law and statutory rules presuming lack of capacity to make a legal contact or to consent to sexual or tortious acts.[7]

The effect of the protection-choice distinction may be illustrated by the situation where a minor child desires state support of a decision to have an abortion. If the physical health of a pregnant minor were in danger in a given case, existing rights to physical protection would prevent parents from legally resisting the abortion. Otherwise, however, no right to protection from serious harm is involved. This leaves the right to make the decision in the choice category.

The long-range psychological implications of the decision present the young woman with formidable difficulties in trying to make a mature assessment of her ability to live with the consequences of either an affirmative or negative abortion decision. However, *there is no reason to assume that she would have greater capacity to evaluate the implications of an abortion than she would the consequences of voting or marrying.* Hafen comments:

> It can be argued, of course, that certain parents may be in no better position to evaluate these risks than are their children—and may be even less likely to provide a better evaluation than a physician or a trained social worker. Whether the adult advice received by a pregnant minor comes from a parent or a professional, however, raises larger questions than who knows more about abortions, since once children are allowed to decide whose advice about abortions they will accept, there is little reason not to extend the right to parental noninterference to many other subjects, ranging from a minor's lifestyle choices to adolescent marriage.[8]

Therefore, to bar a parent's right to prevent a minor child from having an abortion—when no serious danger to health exists—is to provide precedent for denying traditional parental control over the entire range of minor's choice rights. Moreover, the effects of binding, childish choices can create permanent deprivations and state intrusions into the family far more detrimental than the temporary limitations upon the child's freedom.

Moreover, it must be stated with clarity that many of the rights advocated by the children's liberation factions have traditionally been *a moral rather than a legal duty of parents.* For example, the "right" to be prepared for the responsibilities of adulthood is not a legal right of children, but a moral duty of parents. And although it is possible that a child may enforce this duty in the courts, this does not mean it is a right children possess. Instead, it stands only as an unfulfilled moral duty of the parent.

WHAT RIGHTS?

Thus, children do have rights. However, *no rights are absolute.* All rights have limitations.

This has been true even with the most basic human right—the right to life. Traditionally, one who is convicted of taking another's life forfeits his own right to life. This fact is also true of parental rights. And, as we have seen, it is true of any rights a child may claim.

We know from tradition what rights parents possess. However, the rights of children have been blurred over the centuries. With the rise of the children's liberation movement, an assertive campaign has emerged in behalf of the rights of children. As asserted, these rights are *against* traditional parental and family authority.

A basic assumption of children's liberation is that parental rights are derivative. That is, as New York University law professor David A. J. Richards argues, the rights of parents stem "from the presumption that parents have the ability and the willingness that best fulfills *each child's right to individualized care.*"[9] According to Richards, parents have rights, but only "insofar as they do not impinge on the rights of children."[10] He further notes:

> Liberation therefore respects the capacity of parents to realize themselves in child-rearing if their actions are consistent with a proper concern and respect for the developmental rights of children. . . . [T]he parental right has such

> limits, which may be justly enforced when parents transgress [children's rights].[11]

This is an antiparent philosophy—whether it is intended so or not—in that it subordinates parental authority to ensuring the rights of children. This philosophy is reflected in other children's liberation literature, particularly the writings of such advocates as Richard Farson, whose views we considered briefly in an earlier chapter. Farson has emerged as a leading advocate of the complete liberation of children from traditional restraints.

Farson in his book *Birthrights*[12] argues that children possess ten categories of *choice* rights. There is some truth in almost all things. This is true of Farson's categories. But logic renders some of Farson's concepts absurd.

First is the *right of self-determination.* Farson writes:

> Children, like adults should have the right to decide the matters which affect them most directly. The issue of self-determination is at the heart of children's liberation. It is, in fact, the only issue, a definition of the entire concept. The acceptance of the child's right to self-determination is fundamental to all the rights of which children are entitled.[13]

The following rights are of self-determination:

> Children would . . . have the right to exercise determination in decisions about eating, sleeping, playing, listening, reading, washing, and dressing. They would have the right to choose their associates, the opportunity to decide what life goals they wish to pursue, and the freedom to engage in whatever activities are permissible for adults.[14]

Moreover, the "right to self-determination is the right to a single standard of morals and behavior for children and adults. No more double standards."[15] As such, Farson notes:

> Children would have the right to engage in acts which are now acceptable for adults but not for children, and they would not be required to gain permission to do something if such permission is automatically granted adults.[16]

The child, then, is adultified. "The achievement of children's rights," Farson argues, "*must apply to children of all ages,* from birth to adulthood."[17]

Moreover, with the advent of children's rights, "the parent will not have authoritarian control upon which to rely."[18] Instead, the parent "will have to depend more heavily on judgment, advice, and persuasion."[19]

The rights of self-determination are traditional choice rights which hinge on the capacity to exercise mature judgment. Farson assumes capacity is intact even in the small child.

However, no rational society in the history of the Christian West has ever held to such views of children. Besides being nonsensical, Farson's view can be harmful to children. As any parent knows, unless children are *protected* in terms of eating, sleeping, dressing, and the like, they will be inadequately cared for.

The second area is *the right to alternative home environments*. Farson writes:

> [T]he ability to conceive a child gives one no right to raise that child, and that raising a child gives one no right to dominate or to abuse him. The decisions about a child's home environment should not belong to his parents alone. The child must have some right to choose also. . . .
>
> Although the child cannot choose his parents in the genetic sense, he should be able to choose them in the environmental sense. The child cannot avoid deriving his genetic makeup from his parents, but he should have the opportunity, if he chooses, to avoid their daily influence. He must be provided with alternatives to his parents' home environment.[20]

This is true, according to Farson, because "parents are not all that necessary or beneficial for children."[21] Also, "while the natural parents of the child do not necessarily make the best parents, *it is abundantly clear that they make the worst ones.*"[22]

Again, we are dealing with choice, not protection rights. Breaking with the natural parent to live with someone else is, of course, a much more significant break than one dealing with the "right" to eat or sleep when one chooses. Moreover, because such an exercise of choice may be resisted by parents, the state must become involved. As Farson writes, "if he is too young to choose, *his rights must be protected by having an advocate acting in his behalf.*"[23]

Key here, as with the self-determination, are the issues of maturity and capacity. Also evident is the propensity of exploitation. Caring parents keep their children in the confines of the home to protect them from an adult world that will use and harm them.

The right to responsive design is the third category. This concerns accommodating society to the children's size and to their need for safe space.

Farson suggests various devices for miniaturizing society. For example, he suggests that it "would be possible to redesign supermarket shelves in the form of bins mounted on a ferris wheel-like arrangement which the small child . . . could pull down to obtain the item he desired."[24]

On the safety side of things, Farson argues that toys "are among the main weapons in the conspiracy against children."[25] He notes that the "automobile is the number one enemy of children."[26] Most people, I presume, want maximum safety. However, forcing everyone to ride bicycles because children are immobile is again absurd. None of these concerns have been considered as human rights.

More ominous is Farson's argument for medical care for children:

> With respect to children's rights, perhaps the most important change in health care should be the child's right to obtain medical treatment on his own, *without parental consent.*[27]

Clearly, if a parent is denying a child *necessary* medical care, the child should have an option to seek such treatment without the parent's consent. This would fall within the purview of protection rights and, as such, appropriate state enforcement is permissible.

However, if such is not the case, and the child is seeking medical treatment for abortion or other areas affecting the rights of parents, then such should not be protected by law.

Fourth, there is *the right of information.* The argument is that children must have the right to *all* information ordinarily available to adults. This would include information usually censored from young eyes.

Farson, for example, is concerned about censorship in libraries. He writes that "[m]ost libraries for example, do not subscribe to *Playboy*, even though it is one of America's leading magazines."[28] Moreover, if "one expects to find erotic books in the libraries' censored material, he will be disappointed."[29]

To the traditional statement that children should be protected from many types of "adult" information, Farson replies: "Children do not warrant such protection, first because they are not innocent, and second, because it inevitably leads to innocuous, noncontroversial and unstimulating literature."[30]

Again, we are dealing with choice rights which pivot on capacity and maturity. However, Farson's concern that children have a right of access to information in schools has some validity,[31] except where it might transgress upon parental authority.

Fifth is the *right to educate oneself*. This is an argument for the child to choose any form of education he or she wishes, including the option of not attending any kind of school.

Farson's attack on the compulsory education system is admirable, even if it is partly for the wrong reasons. He writes: "Compulsory education and the autocracy fostered by it has robbed children of every sense of what independence of action and freedom of choice might be."[32] Also, "[a]t a time when we need acceptance of diversity, we teach uniformity."[33]

However, Farson argues that within the right to educate oneself is the "freedom from indoctrination."[34] He writes:

> Children are seen as fair game for the imposition of almost any value system held by an adult who works or lives with them. . . . This is seen as an inviolable parental right. As a result, countless children experience a rape of the mind. . . . The worst situations center around the teaching of religion.[35]

And, of course, "[i]ndoctrination will also be minimized when parents and teachers become less powerful . . . and children are given their rights in all our institutions."[36]

The United States Supreme Court and lower courts have on numerous occasions recognized the right of parents to direct the spiritual education and upbringing of their children.[37] This fact, as we noted earlier, has long been recognized by the Christian West as part of parental authority.

The troublesome question arises when parents fail, or even refuse, to educate their children. Unfortunately, Farson's argument can have the side effect of "liberating" parents from the moral duty to educate their children.

Sixth, there is the argument that children have *the right to freedom from physical punishment*. The assertion is that children should live free of physical threat from those who are larger and more powerful than they. Farson writes:

> [C]orporal punishment violates children's rights. It deprives the child of the right to life, liberty, and property without due process of law. It cannot be condoned under any circumstances, *even if it did "work."* For this reason alone, it must be eliminated from the arsenal of weapons used against children to force their compliance and submission to authority.[38]

Any right children would have in terms of corporal punishment would be the freedom from what has traditionally been assault and battery. Assault and battery is at least a misdemeanor in every state. As such, it would fall under the rights of protection.

Besides the Biblical admonition to use corporal punishment to discipline children, there appears to be a recognized need for a limited use of spanking. The United States Supreme Court has recognized its use in public schools with limitations.[39] Moreover, in 1969 the National Education Association surveyed its membership of professional educators, finding that 65 percent of the elementary educators and 55 percent of the secondary educators favored it. In Pittsburgh, 70 percent of the teachers signed a petition asking for a ban on spanking to be lifted.[40]

The right to sexual freedom is the seventh category. Farson advocates that children should have the right to conduct their sexual lives with no more restriction than adults.

This clearly falls within choice rights. It is utterly dependent upon maturity and capacity to understand the nature of sexual acts. Traditionally children, except for certain lapses in history, have been shielded from the world of sex. In our contemporary sexually charged society, children are introduced to the idea of sex in their early years.

The children's liberation movement argues for much more, however. Farson argues that the "first aspect of child's right to sexual freedom is his right to information about sex. . . . [that is] to have access to *any* information available to *any* adults."[41] This means eliminating "*all* forms of censorship which keep children ignorant about sex and giving them access *to all* of the information to which adults have access."[42] Farson continues:

> Much to the discomfort of adults, it would also include the right to enter stores and theaters where "adults only" films, magazines, and other sexual entertainment is presented. Pornography is neither one of the best nor one of the most common sources of sex information, but we must recognize it as an important source, even if we find it personally distasteful. Although the pictures of sex which one receives from pornography are at least as distorted as those from public school sex education, they can provide many answers which the child simply does not get from adults.[43]

The right to sexual freedom also means eliminating stereotypes:

> We may have greatly overestimated the differences between males and females. There are obvious biological differences: Men impregnate; women menstruate, conceive and lactate, but there may not be too many other differences that are not culturally learned. Children's bodies are different only in genitalia. Girls behave differently from boys mainly because of social learning.[44]

Further, "myths" must be dispelled—"that adult-child sex usually forces physical violence and sexual activity on an unwilling child. That is not true. In many instances, the child is a willing participant."[45]

This also means rethinking prohibitions against incest:

> Incest and sexual activity within the family, whether it be father-daughter, mother-son, brother-sister or any homosexual combination of those partners, is far more common and far less traumatic than we have always been led to believe. Perhaps no activity is more tabooed in our society, yet current estimates of the number of Americans who have been involved in incestuous experience run as high as twenty million; that is, one in every ten people. Studies of incest reveal that the dangers have been highly overrated.[46]

For Farson, sex can begin very early. "Almost everyone has difficulty accepting the fact that children are not only sensual but sexual, and that some are capable of sexual activity almost from birth."[47]

In a day and age when children are sexually exploited and abused, it is difficult to understand arguments for adultifying children in terms of sex. It can only result in harm.

Eighth, *the right to economic power* is advocated. Children, as the argument goes, should have the right to work, to acquire and manage money, to receive equal pay for equal work, to gain promotions to leadership positions, to own property, to develop a credit record, to enter into binding contracts, to engage in enterprise, to obtain guaranteed support apart from the family, and to achieve financial independence.[48]

These are choice rights. It has been universally recognized that children, because of immaturity, cannot engage in business transactions or enter into binding contracts. In fact, the child labor laws came into being because children of the nineteenth century who entered the business world were grossly exploited. Placing such rights in children, then, is not only unrealistic but would, in the end, be harmful to young people.

The right to political power is listed ninth. The idea is that children should possess the same political rights in voting, holding office, and the like. Farson writes:

> The major fear is that the children's vote will be reckless, selfish, and irresponsible. It is, however, difficult to believe that children would vote more irresponsibly than adults have voted. Even if children voted for a big rock candy

> mountain, it would hardly outdo adults for ridiculous expenditures.[49]

Should a child have the "right to hold high office"? "Again the answer is yes. A person cannot be denied the right to seek and hold office simply because of age."[50]

Choice rights are involved here. No one who lives with at least one foot in reality believes small children should vote or hold national political offices.

Finally, Farson argues for the *right to justice*. Children under this category must have the guarantee of a fair trial with due process of law, an advocate to protect their rights against parents as well as the system, and a uniform standard of detention.

The basic propositions here are protection rights which are the basis of the juvenile court system. The great danger in adultifying children is that they may be placed on the same level as adult criminals. At this point the child loses protection and the parents lose their children—especially if children have the right to an advocate or lawyer.

In summary, children do have rights. Moreover, parents have a moral duty to treat their children as children in not taking their childhood from them. Parents also have a moral duty to care for, protect, and love their children. Parents, moreover, have a duty to treat their children with worth and dignity and to ensure their children the right to life (whether unborn or born). Otherwise, all traditional distinctions are lost. As a result, both parent and child are harmed.

ABANDONING CHILDREN TO THEIR RIGHTS

Children have special needs that must be met in their movement toward maturity and independence. The most critical of these needs, as some have recognized, is a satisfactory and permanent psychological relationship with their parents.[51]

Thus, even though we may establish as our highest priority the meeting of these needs, "the worst possible results would be visited upon children by 'liberating' them from the crucial psychological matrix of true family relationships."[52] That kind of liberation would constitute the most ironic adult treatment of children—"abandoning them to their rights." As the psychologists tell us:

> To safeguard the right of parents to raise their children as they see fit, free of government intrusion, except in cases of neglect and abandonment, is to safeguard each child's need for continuity. This preference for minimum state intervention and for leaving well enough alone is reinforced by our recognition that law is incapable of effectively managing except in a very gross sense, so delicate and complex a relationship as that between parent and child.[53]

This suggests that parental authority must be regarded *"as a sovereign right"* if the basic psychological needs of children are to be met.[54] If the relationship fails, either because of state intervention or because a parent has substantial doubts about the extent of his or her personal authority over the child, serious psychological defiencies and harm are likely to exist.

Any denial of parental authority, unless it is based upon traditional limitations, necessarily adds to the authority of children. Clearly, too much freedom for children can undermine and finally destroy the fundamental institutions of our society, as well as the human relationships that sustain them.

THIRTEEN

TO BE HUMAN

Particularly since World War II, many changes have occurred in family patterns and child-rearing in the United States. However, their essence may be conveyed in a single sentence: *Children used to be brought up by their parents.*[1]

Over the years, *de facto* responsibility for the upbringing of children has shifted away from the family to other settings in the society—such as state and private institutions and individuals who attempt to simulate the original family setting (for example, foster parents). Some of these do not recognize or accept the task, and when they do recognize it they do not perform the task well.

However, the basic problems are within the natural family itself. As Cornell University professor Urie Bronfenbrenner writes:

> While the family still has the primary moral and legal responsibility for the character development of children, it often lacks the power or opportunity to do the job, primarily because *parents and children no longer spend enough time together in those situations in which such training is possible.* This is not because parents do not want to spend time with their children. It is simply that conditions have changed.[2]

The crisis, thus, in what we have termed "parental rights" can be summed up by saying that *Americans have,* in the traditional sense, *ceased being parents.* In the process, a new class of people—children with the state as their protector—has emerged.

CHANGING STRUCTURES

To begin with, families used to be bigger—not in terms of more children so much as more adults. This included grandparents, uncles, aunts, cousins. Moreover, those relatives who did not live with the family lived nearby.

There were community visits, dinners, and get-togethers. People knew one another, all of them—the old folk, the middle-aged, the older cousins. And what's more, they knew everyone else. This had its good side and its bad side:

> On the good side, some of these relatives were interesting people, or so you thought at the time. Uncle Charlie had been to China. Aunt Sue made the best penuche fudge on the block. Cousin Bill could read people's minds (he claimed). And they all gave you presents.
>
> But there was the other side. You had to give them all Christmas presents. Besides, everybody minded your business. They wanted to know where you had been, where you were going, and why. And if they did not like what they heard, they said so (particularly if you had told the truth).[3]

But it may not simply be one's relatives. Everybody in the neighborhood minded each other's business. Again, this had two aspects.

Children were watched by people in the neighborhood. If they walked on the railroad trestle, the phone rang at their parents' house. Children also had the run of the neighborhood. Children could, without the parents worrying, play in the park, go to the store, the lumberyard and so on.

Although these are now only memories, they still have their present-day vestiges. In fact, research has systematically documented important facets of American neighborhood life. These investigations compared daily life of children growing up in a small community with those living in larger towns. The principal difference is: unlike their urban and suburban age-mates, children in a small town become well acquainted with a substantially greater number of adults in different walks of life, and are more likely to be active participants in adult settings which they enter.[4]

The stable world of the small town has been absorbed by an ever-shifting suburbia. As a consequence, children are growing up in a different kind of environment. Urbanization has reduced the extended trustee family to a nuclear, atomistic one *with only two adults*. The functioning neighborhood—where it has not decayed into an urban or rural slum—has withered to a small circle of friends, most of them accessible only by car or telephone. Pardoxically, although there are more people around, *there are fewer opportunities for meaningful human contact.*

Whereas previously the world in which the child lived consisted of a diversity of people in a diversity of settings, now for millions of American children the neighborhood is nothing but row upon row of buildings where "other people" live. One house or apartment is much like another—and so are the people. As Bronfenbrenner writes:

> They all have more or less the same income, and the same way of life. But the child does not see much of that life, for all that people do in the neighborhood is to come home to it, have a drink, eat dinner, mow the lawn, watch television, and sleep. Increasingly often, today's housing projects have no stores, no shops, no services, no adults at work or play. This is the sterile world in which many of our children grow, and this is the "urban renewal" we offer to the families we would rescue from the slums.[5]

The entire concept of the neighborhood is lost. Rarely can a child see people working at their trades. Everyone is out of sight. Nor can the child listen to the gossip at the post office or on the park bench. And there are no abandoned houses, no barns, no attics to break into. It is a pretty bland world for children to grow up in.

It does not really matter anyway. Children are not home

either. They leave early on the school bus and it is about dinner-time when they get back. Also, there may not be anybody home when they get there. "If the mother is not working, at least part-time . . . she is out a lot because of social obligations—not just to be with friends, but to do things for the community. The men leave in the morning before the children are up. And they do not get back until after the children have eaten supper. Fathers are often away weekends, as well as during the week."[6]

All this means that American parents do not spend as much time with children as they used to. Systematic evidence consistent with this conclusion comes from a survey by professor Bronfenbrenner of changes in child-rearing practices in the United States over a twenty-five-year period.[7] The data was interpreted as indicating a trend toward universal permissiveness in parent-child relations, especially in the period after World War II. He notes: "The generalization applies in such diverse areas as oral behavior, toilet accidents, dependency, sex aggressiveness, and freedom of movement outside of the house."[8]

Years later, however, Bronfenbrenner recognized that the data admitted of another interpretation, consistent with the parental trend toward permissiveness, but going beyond it. Namely, he writes: "The same facts could be viewed as reflecting *a progressive decrease,* especially in recent decades, *in the amount of contact between* American *parents and their children.*"[9]

This is true despite the fact that other countries and cultures, including the Soviet Union, allegedly have better relations and more intimate contact with their children.[10] American society, therefore, emerges as one that gives decreasing prominence and importance to the family as a *socializing* agent.

This is a by-product of a variety of changes, all operating to decrease the prominence and power of the family in the lives of children. These social changes include "[u]rbanization, child labor laws, the abolishment of the apprentice system, commuting, centralized schools, zoning ordinances, the working mother, the experts' advice to be permissive, the seductive power of television for keeping children occupied, the delegation and professionalization of child care."[11] All of these manifestations of "progress" have operated to decrease opportunity for contact between children and parents, or, for that matter, adults in general. As a result, *parents and children have become strangers.*

AT THE SCHOOLHOUSE

If a child is not with his parents or other adults, where does he spend his time? *He or she is with other children*—in school, after school, over weekends, and on holidays.

However, even this contact is further restricted. The passing of the neighborhood school in favor of "educational advantages" made possible by consolidation, homogenous grouping by age, and more recently by "ability" has set the pattern for other activities. Thus, from preschool days onward, a child's contacts with other children in school, camp, and neighborhood tend to be limited to youngsters of his own age and social background. Very clearly, *we are moving very rapidly toward a society that is segregated not only by race and class, but also by age.*

Amazingly enough, this age segregation occurs everywhere, even in institutions that have traditionally encouraged relationships across age lines. Church Sunday schools, for example, are invariably grouped in such categories as: preschool, early grades, teens, singles, young married, adults, over 65s and so on. These types of groups effectively destroy relationships between the younger and older people. Is it any wonder that there is a lack of "community" in churches and Christian groups?

Much of this age-segregation mentality has been provided us by the public education system. Mass *compulsory* education, besides whatever benefits it has bestowed upon American culture, has been a destructive force for several basic reasons.

Built on the nineteenth-century factory model, mass public education taught basic reading, writing, and arithmetic, a bit of theory, and other subjects. Alvin Toffler in *The Third Wave* states:

> This was the "overt curriculum." But beneath it lay an invisible or "covert curriculum" that was far more basic. It consisted—and still does in most industrial nations—of three courses; one in punctuality, one in obedience, and one in rote, repetitive work. Factory labor demanded workers who showed up on time, especially assembly-line

> hands. It demanded workers who would take orders from a management hierarchy without questioning. And it demanded men and women prepared to slave away at machines or in offices, performing brutally repetitious operations.[12]

Therefore, from the midnineteenth century on, one found a relentless educational progression. Children started school at a younger and younger age, the school year became longer and longer (it climbed 35 percent between 1878 and 1956), and the number of years of compulsory education schooling increased.[13] However, this had a profound effect on family patterns.

> By setting up mass education systems, governments not only helped to machine youngsters for their future roles in the industrial work force (hence, in effect, subsidizing industry) but also simultaneously encouraged the spread of the nuclear family form. By relieving the family of educational and other traditional functions, governments accelerated the adaptation of family structure to the needs of the factory system.[14]

Mass compulsory education also rigorously promoted a uniform and therefore monolithic approach to education. With the older one-room schoolhouse, all ages interacted. With mass education, segregation by ages began. Moreover, classroom materials and curriculum became more uniform and monolithic. The *diversity* of earlier educational experience was lost.

The mass educational system produced the professional educator. This new type of educator not only allegedly knew more about education, but in the end *replaced the parent as the educator of children.*

Thus, as a state-financed institution the public education system began more and more to duplicate, and eventually replace, many family functions. For example, a basic function of the family from time immemorial had been the education of the child. Another basic function was socialization. However, as parents began sharing their children with the state, these functions and others have been lost. This has progressed to the point where the state can claim it is, at least, a parent (and often a conflicting parent) of the child.

Mass state education has forced children into horizontal peer relationships, thereby abrogating the traditional vertical relationships with adults. It is here that a major part of the *socialization* process has been assumed by the public schools. As a consequence, there has been a move away from parental relationships to peer relationships along with all the trappings of "peer pressure."

Compulsory public education produces a peer group that occupies a place of primary importance in the life of the student. As professor James Coleman has noted:

> This setting-apart of our children in schools—which take on ever more functions, ever more "extracurricular activities"—for an ever larger period of training has a singular impact on the child of the high-school age. He is "cut-off" from the rest of society, forced inward toward his own age group, made to carry out his whole social life with others his own age. With his fellows, he comes to constitute a small society, one that has most of its important interactions *within* itself, and maintains only a few threads of connection with the outside adult society.[15]

In essence, this means that the primary relationship is not parent-child or, for that matter, even child-child. Instead, it is child-state in that the parental vacuum has been filled by the state-controlled public education system. Indeed, a primary function of public education, as sociologists argue, is to provide for a "uniform orientation at the societal level."[16]

A negative effect of public education socialization is its persistent conformity. Conformity to behavior and beliefs of fellow-students is at very best strong. Sometimes conformity becomes an obsessive drive of students. It almost always has a harmful effect on parent-child relations.

A further negative effect is that the rare nonconforming student who attempts to withstand such socialization pressures is generally, as psychological and sociological studies show, rejected as a deviant or stigmatized in various ways. This can have severe emotional effects on such students when religious beliefs are involved. In fact, one research study indicates that "doubting religious doctrines is the source of much mental anguish and emotional stress on the part of the adolescent."[17] And, of course, the religious student faces this more and more since the full-blown arrival of the fateful separation of church and state doctrine, which, as it freed the state schools from teaching religion, also fragmented the process of education.

ALIENATION

Mass statist education, with the urbanization process and other societal forces, has simply alienated child and parent-adults. For example, one study of 766 sixth-grade children indicated that children, during a weekend, spent an average of two or three hours a day with their parents. Over the same period, they spent more time than this with groups of friends. In short, they spent about twice as much time with peers, either singly or in groups, as with their parents.[18]

Moreover, their behavior apparently reflects preference as well as practice. "When asked with whom they would rather spend a free weekend afternoon," writes Bronfenbrenner, "many more chose friends than parents."[19]

Analysis of the data on the child's perception of his parents, his peers, and himself has led researchers to conclude that "peer-oriented" children were more influenced by a *lack* of attention and concern at home than by the attractiveness of the peer group. "In general, the peer-oriented children held rather negative views of themselves and the peer group. They also expressed a dim view of their own future."[20]

Finally, peer-oriented children report engaging in more antisocial behavior such as "doing something illegal," "playing hooky," lying, teasing other children, and the like. In summary:

> *[I]t would seem that the peer-oriented child is more a product of parental disregard than of the attractiveness of the peer group*—that he turns to his age-mates less by choice than by default. The vacuum left by the withdrawal of parents and adults from the lives of children is filled with an undesired—and possibly *undesirable*—substitute of any age-segregated peer group.[21]

However, we must not forget that it is an age-segregation we have programmed them for by the very practices of our major institutions, including the church.

Looking forward, then, we can anticipate increased alienation, indifference, antagonism, and violence on the part of the younger generation in all segments of society—middle-class children as well as the "disadvantaged." Thus, if parents do not once again become involved in the lives of their children, there is trouble ahead for American society.

SOME SOLUTIONS

Our child-free society does not produce happy or well-balanced people. The high rate of suicide in all age categories is evidence of this.

But how do we deal with problems in the family in terms of parental authority? How can we preserve the basic rights of parents to care for, protect, discipline, and nurture their children toward a responsible independence?

The answer to what seems a perplexing problem can be summed up in one sentence: *We must have better families.* And this can be done by returning the basic functions of parenting to the families once again. It also means returning children to the world of adults in restructuring adult-child relationships.

A basic function of parents that must be recovered from the state is *education.* The assembly-line education of both the state and private (including Christian) schools must be rethought.

The idea that only "professional" educators are qualified to teach children is a myth perpetuated by the educational establishment. Another more absurd myth is the concept that teachers must be certified by the state in order to be qualified to teach. The men and women who built this country were essentially home-taught by either their "uncertified, nonprofessional" parents or tutors that assisted their parents.

The family can recover the education function again. In some ways this is happening today. Primarily it is happening through the flowering home school movement and "parent-run" private schools. Christian schools that are not parent-run are falling into the same trap as the state schools in usurping the function of the family. This can be easily remedied by putting parents in control of the school. This does not mean merely having parent meetings at the school. It means having parents on the school board and heavily involved in every aspect of the school. Otherwise, even private Christian schools can tend to be antiparent.

If at all possible, Christian and other private schools should cooperate with those parents teaching their children in the home. Christian schools can allow home education parents the use of their facilities as well as allow home education children to take certain courses of instruction at the school.

Moreover, Christian schools and churches should work closely with home education parents in getting state laws amended to allow for home education. Also, compulsory education laws should be altered to allow children to spend less hours in formal schooling. Children should be encouraged to spend more time at home with their parents. There is much "dead-time" during the school day, and if this could be eliminated less time at the school building would be required.

TO BE HUMAN

Children need people in order to reach full human potential. Isolation of children from adults simultaneously threatens the growth of the individual and the survival of the society. *Childrearing is not something children can do for themselves.* Bronfenbrenner writes:

> It is primarily through observing, playing, and working with others older and younger than himself that a child discovers both what he can do and who he can become—that he develops both his ability and his identity. It is primarily through exposure and interaction with adults and children of different ages that a child acquires new interests and skills and learns the meaning of tolerance, cooperation, and compassion. Hence to relegate children to a world of their own is to deprive them of their humanity, and ourselves as well.[22]

What *we are experiencing* in America today is *a breakdown in the process of making human beings human.* "By isolating our children from the rest of society, we abandon them to a world devoid of adults and ruled by the destructive impulses and controlling pressures both of the age-segregated peer group and the aggressive and exploitive television screen, we leave our children bereft of standards and support and our own lives impoverished and corrupted."[23]

We have simply reversed our priorities. Other things have become more important than children. It is a betrayal of our children. It underlines the ever-increasing disillusionment and alienation among young people in all segments of American society.

Those who grew up in settings where children and families still counted are able to react to the frustrations of modern secular society in positive ways. Parents and families are a part of their lives.

However, those who came from situations in which families and children were a low priority are striking out. The alienated child, for whatever reason, sets up his or her parents and societies as objects of resistance.

Thus, it is the family that builds productive people. This means, again, that parents and children must be together. It also means that parents and children should be with each other in the family setting as much as possible. Thus, parents should do what some may consider to be old-fashioned; that is, *keep their children at home,* and away from all the extracurricular activities that tend to disrupt families today.

On the other hand, parents must keep themselves within the family environment. Fathers and mothers who are workaholics are not good parents. This is more so with mothers.

All current trends point to the increasing participation of women and *mothers* in the work force.[24] One may disagree that women are more gifted and effective in the care of young children than are men. However, the fact remains that in our society today, it is overwhelmingly on the women, and especially mothers, that the care of our children depends.

Contrary to what modern feminism may say, the most important function any human being serves is that of being a mother. With the working mother, however, the richness of the traditional family suffers and in many instances is lost. Children deprived of a mother because she works (unless absolutely essential) are children who have been robbed. It is not too satisfying to be a "latch-key" child. The child must have the security that only a mother can give. And if she is absent, the chances are that insecurity will develop.

There are instances when it is necessary that mothers work. If so, there are numerous in-home employment opportunities for mothers. Or fathers and mothers who wish to be close to their children could both work out of the home and split the work hours. Moreover, part-time work for mothers is another option and is much preferable to the full-time "career mother."

There is one *caveat,* however. Mothers with *small* children should avoid working. Mothers have their greatest impact with young children. And small children need mother-contact in their early years.

With the withdrawal of societal support of the family, women and mothers have become increasingly isolated. An increasing responsibility for the care and upbringing of children has fallen on the young mother. Under some circumstances, it is not surprising that many young women in America are in the process of revolting. I, for one, understand and share their sense of rage. However, I fear that the consequences of the solutions advocated by the radical feminists will have the effect of isolating children still further from the kind of care and attention they need. Again, the ideal arrangement for the development of parent-child relations may be one in which the mother and also the father work part-time. In the process, there are shared responsibilities for the care of children.

If parents cannot begin to increase the time they spend with their children, then the "alienation gap" is going to increase. As a result, children will become even more estranged. Simply put, it is much easier to assert children's rights against parents who are strangers.

HOW CAN THE CHRISTIAN COMMUNITY HELP?

One point must be made abundantly clear. *The properly functioning Christian family is the central source of power and social energy in any society.*

Because the Christian family, in its true trustee form, is the great locale of power, it has often incurred the enmity of other claimants to power. One of these has been the church.

The older asceticism, because of misinterpretation of certain "celibacy" passages in the Bible, saw marital life as a lower way of life and at times showed no little hostility toward the family. This attitude is still present in many evangelical churches in a disguised form. The family is, in effect, "saved" from itself by being drawn into the church night after night for church activities. At one time, for example, "church elders made annual visitation of all homes to ensure that the children were taught their catechism, and that the family prayer and Bible study was the practice."[25] Today the effort is directed towards attendance at weekday church prayer meetings and Bible study. The center, therefore, has shifted.

However, the center should be reshifted back to the family again. The local church should stress the importance of the family as *the* center of worship, education, and development of human beings—that is, the center of power.

This necessarily means that church and pastor must loosen their authoritarian control over parishioners and, especially, families. It also means decreasing activities that tear parents and children away from the home.

These principles should be taught in the church. Moreover, the church, as a teaching institution, should provide families with the necessary instruction and educational materials on developing strong families. Therefore, a central effort of local churches should be in building up families.

Contrary to what some may think, this will not weaken local churches. In fact, the opposite is true. Strong families make strong churches.

Concern for the family goes beyond the churches. Other Christian organizations, no matter their professed purposes, should have as a central function strengthening the family units of those who work for and with them. Many Christian organizations, because of their zeal to "win the world for Jesus," are hurting families.

The entire "jet-setting" mentality of modern Christianity is harmful. The evangelists and Christian "celebrities" who have families and who are on the road more than they are home with their wives and children are not doing the "Lord's work" in the truest sense. The basic ministry of a father and a mother is their family. Saving the world but losing your children is a heavy price to pay for fulfillment of big egoes. It hurts everyone.

Priorities are, thus, the key. Do we want to be with our families, or do we want to attend the endless string of "Christian" seminars and conferences that too often occur on weekends (when parents should be with their children)?

STRANGERS IN THE LAND

If parents and adults will commit themselves to restructuring the family and caring for children, then the children, who have become strangers in the land, will return. If not, the entire area of parental authority and parental rights will worsen.

As you look in the steely cold eyes of a child who is completely estranged and is battling his parents and others, remember that there may have been a time when this confrontation could have been avoided. To do so requires commitment—commitment to people in pursuing a better future for all of God's children.

PART FIVE

PRACTICALITIES

Now the window is open and we must take advantage of it in every way we can as citizens, as Christian citizens of the democracy in which we still have freedom.

Francis A. Schaeffer
A Christian Manifesto (1981)

FOURTEEN

PRACTICAL CONSIDERATIONS

In recent years there have been a number of proposed model statutes concerning the grounds for the termination of parental rights. Most of these proposals would allow greater discretion to judges to terminate the parent-child relationship.

For example, the model act drafted by the National Council of Juvenile Court Judges (1976) allows the court to consider a variety of nebulous, nonexclusive factors in deciding the issue of parental unfitness, including such things as the "emotional neglect of the child."[1] Under the Katz Model Act (1978), a child may be deemed "abused or neglected" and the parents' rights therefore terminated when the child's "physical or mental health is harmed or threatened with harm by the acts of omissions of his parent."[2] The term "harm" is broadly defined to include the infliction of "mental injury."[3]

Clearly, a fundamental concept of modern culture is that the rights of parents are limited—in certain cases *very* limited. Moreover, many parents sense a certain "fear" or "hesitation" when dealing with their children. This is especially so, for example, in public places, when it comes to correcting or disciplining their children.

Therefore, what was once considered normal is now considered aberrant. With the focus on the best interests of the child, parents, when problems arise in the family, are often automatically suspect. This means that about anyone in our culture can become an informer against parents. Let me cite two examples that the author was personally involved in.

One case involved a mother who was shopping in a store. While standing in the checkout lane, she refused her three-year-old child's request for a candy bar. The child threw a temper tantrum. The mother swatted the child several times on the behind. She paid for the items she bought by check.

Shortly after she arrived home, a social worker came to the house and demanded to inspect the child for possible marks and bruises. The charge was child abuse.

The mother had been reported to the welfare department by the store clerk, who obtained her address from the check.

The surprised mother allowed the welfare worker to strip her child in her home. The worker found no bruises or even red marks, but demanded that the mother, with her husband, would have to come to counseling services once a week for at least one year. Sessions there would concern proper parenting.

The second situation, which occurred in another state, involved a conversation between two young teenage girls whose homes were close enough to converse from upper-story windows. One girl, who was in a strong Christian family, indicated that she was not, along with other restrictions, allowed to attend movies. This infuriated the other girl, whose mother telephoned the state welfare department. The welfare department then conducted an investigation at the child's home to see if this was a case of child abuse.

Both of these instances were resolved short of going to court. However, they are not isolated instances. There are a long train of stories where neighbors, store clerks, and the like have become informers to the state against legitimate parental actions.

WHAT TO DO?

There are certain practical actions that can be taken to preserve parental authority and parental liberty.

First, the *individual parents* should, besides working to have a stable relationship with their children, educate themselves on the entire range of parent-child-state issues facing them. The materials cited in this book, along with others, should be read and studied.

Parents should familiarize themselves with *all* state laws concerning parents' rights. Parents should also, if possible, retain a competent local attorney. This means having an attorney prior to any contact from the state. Thus, if and when parents are contacted by state officials attempting to "investigate," such officials can be referred to their lawyer. Under no circumstances should parents dialogue with state officials or allow them to inspect either their children or home. They should simply be referred to the attorney involved.

Concerned parent organizations should be formed. These groups could organize educational activities, such as seminars and conferences. They could act as representatives of individual parents who have grievances with the public schools or who have been contacted by state agencies attempting to intervene in family affairs.

Once formed, concerned parent organizations could hire attorneys to either defend or prosecute lawsuits. They could lobby their legislatures and local governing bodies on laws and key issues.

Concerned parent organizations should coordinate with existing Christian school organizations and other groups to assist parents engaged in home education. Many times such people have no place to turn to.

The possibilities for concerned parent groups are virtually unlimited. Only a lack of imagination limits the possibilities.

THE CHURCH

The *local church* should be the strongest, most visible supporter of families. The church certainly should in no way detract from the family.

This will necessarily mean limiting church activities that remove the parents from the home. Instead, parents should be encouraged to spend time with the children.

The church should present, on an intermittent but continuing basis, solid teaching on parental responsibilities as well as the responsibilities of children toward their parents. The Bible is very clear on how a family should operate.

Building strong families should be a main focus of the local church. The church should be certain no family within its reach is in need. Besides the usual deacon fund, a family fund should be established to assist families requiring assistance. Moreover, the Christians involved in the local church should commit time to visiting and helping families who require it.

The local church must also take the lead in combatting one of the major concerns of our time: alienation and loneliness. There are within churches many lonely adults. Churches should encourage families to work and fellowship with the singles, the aged, and others in the church. Children, as we discussed earlier, have very few meaningful adult relationships. A program, as described here, could be one way to solve several problems at once.

The local church should also be the first institution to deal with child abuse. If at all possible, the pastor should correct such situations before they warrant state intervention. In this respect, pastors should work with qualified counselors and others who can be trusted to protect the family. The family is too important to leave in the hands of those who do not hold it in high esteem.

ADVOCACY

The major arenas of confrontation in terms of both parents' or children's rights will be the legislatures and the courts.

Legislation can, as we have discussed, be the target of concerned parent organizations. Of course, the best of possible situations would be a complete absence of legislation. The culture should, as it was in early America, be predisposed to parental authority. However, that is not the present reality.

The solution may be the drafting and consideration of model parents' rights legislation. Such legislation could be offered on a state-by-state basis. At that point, concerned parent organizations could oppose or favor the legislation as it is modified in the various redrafting committees in the state legislatures.

However, it must be emphasized that in most instances *no* legislation is preferable to poor legislation. Poorly drafted legislation leaves too much leeway for judicial interpretation.

A well-drafted law protecting parental rights is another story. One important reason is that well-drafted legislation will most likely operate to keep the issue of parental rights out of the courts.

The courts today have abandoned any semblance of the older absolutes. Decisions are often made subjectively by the judge. To use an old metaphor, "it is like rolling dice" to enter a courtroom today, especially in this sensitive area.

This fact necessitates aggressive legal representation of parental rights. Too often Christian attorneys have been willing to compromise in the delicate situations involving parental rights. This attitude has led to some poor results. Advocacy in this area of the law must be aggressive.

Attorneys should also work closely with concerned parent organizations advising and, if necessary, defending or suing on behalf of concerned parent organizations. In any event, the attorneys defending parental rights should be on the offensive, not the defensive.

Finally, for both the layman and the attorney *persistence* must be the rule. Do not give up. If a legislative body, for example, refuses to listen, persist until they relent. This means being organized, but it also means not wavering or compromising.

COMMITMENT TO THE TRUTH

No matter how hard we may work toward becoming involved, passing laws and winning court cases, no one's rights will really be secured unless there is a commitment in at least two directions.

The first is, of course, the commitment to be good parents.[4] As we discussed in Chapter 13, that takes a *total* commitment as parents to the family and, in particular, to children.

Second, as Christians we must be committed to stand strong for the truth. The Good News of Christ must be externalized. Christians must live their faith. They must let the world know that there is true truth. Christians can no longer hide from this fact and expect political freedom to remain intact.

In this true truth, however, is true freedom. True freedom is the inward freedom that only Christ can give. And if it is manifested externally in all areas of life, we will see a marked change in the culture.

Children are the living messages we send to a time we will not see. Hopefully, because of our efforts, they will live free lives unfettered by the oppression that marks our times.

NOTES

Author's Foreword:

1. George Orwell, *Nineteen Eighty-Four* (New York: Harcourt, Brace, World, 1949), pp. 136, 137.
2. *Presidential Proclamation* 5315 (April 4, 1985) (emphasis supplied).

Chapter One

1. *See generally* Neil Postman, *The Disappearance of Childhood* (New York: Delacorte Press, 1982).
2. *In re Welfare of Snyder,* 532 P.2d 278, 279 (S. Ct. Wash. 1975).
3. *Snyder v. State,* 577 P.2d 160, 161 (Wash. App. 1978).
4. *Id.*
5. 532 P.2d at 280.
6. Incorrigible is traditionally defined as: "Incapable of being corrected or amended. . . . Bad or depraved beyond correction or reform." 1 *The Compact Edition of the Oxford English Dictionary* (Oxford: Oxford U. Press, 1971), p. 1408.
7. 532 P.2d at 281.
8. *Id.* at 282.
9. *Webster's New Collegiate Dictionary* (Springfield, Mass.: G. and C. Merriam, 1975), p. 335.
10. 532 P.2d at 281.

Chapter Two

1. Urie Bronfenbrenner, *Two Worlds of Childhood: U.S. and U.S.S.R.* (New York: Russell Sage Foundation, 1970), p. 1.
2. Alvin Toffler, *The Third Wave* (New York: Bantam Books, 1981), pp. 211, 212.
3. *Ibid.*, p. 215.
4. *Ibid. Also see* John W. Whitehead, *The Stealing of America* (Westchester, Ill.: Crossway Books, 1982), pp. 60-72.

5. Vincent De Francis, *Child Abuse—Preview of a Nationwide Survey* (Denver: American Humane Association, 1963).
6. *Ibid.*, pp. 5-7.
7. As cited in Allan H. McCoid, *The Battered Child and Other Assaults Upon the Family: Part One,* 50 Minnesota Law Review 1, 16 (1966).
8. *Ibid.*
9. *Attorney General's Task Force on Family Violence* (September 1984), p. 11 (footnotes omitted).
10. *Ibid.*
11. Neil Postman, *The Disappearance of Childhood* (New York: Delacorte Press, 1982), p. 139.
12. *Ibid.* (emphasis supplied).
13. *See generally* Richard Farson, *Birthrights* (New York: Macmillan, 1974).
14. Patricia Wald, "Making Sense out of the Rights of Youth," 55 *Journal of the Child Welfare League of America* (1976), p. 382.
15. *Ibid.*, pp. 382, 387.
16. *Ibid.*, pp. 383-84.
17. *Ibid.*, p. 386.
18. *Ibid.*
19. *Ibid.*, p. 387 (emphasis supplied).
20. *Ibid.*, p. 386.
21. *Ibid.*, p. 388.
22. *Ibid.*, p. 387.
23. Ted Gest, "The Other Victims of Child Abuse," *U.S. News and World Report* (April 1, 1985), p. 66.
24. *Ibid.*
25. *Ibid.*
26. Al Haas, "The New Victims of Child Abuse," *The Philadelphia Inquirer* (June 9, 1985), p. 6-F.
27. *Ibid.*
28. *Ibid.*
29. *Child Abuse and You. . . ,* p. 1. This is a pamphlet distributed by Childhelp USA, Woodland Hills, California 91370.
30. *Ibid.*, p. 4 (emphasis supplied).
31. *Ibid.*, p. 1.
32. *Ibid.*, p. 6.
33. *Ibid.*
34. *Ibid.*, pp. 7, 8.
35. *New York Family Court Act,* Section 1012 (McKinney Supp. 1983).
36. *Ibid.*, Section 1012(h).
37. *Ibid.*, Section 1011 (emphasis supplied).
38. *Connecticut General Statutes,* Section 466-120 (West Supp. 1985).
39. *Montana Code Annotated,* Section 41-3-102 (Cum. Supp. 1983).
40. *Arizona Revised Statutes,* Section 8-201 (West 1974).
41. *Ibid.*, Section 8-201 (West Supp. 1984).
42. *Idaho Code,* Section 16-1625(j) (Supp. 1974).

43. Lloyd Shearer, "Preventing Sexual Abuse of Children," *Parade* (May 26, 1985), p. 16.

Chapter Three

1. *San Francisco Examiner* (Nov. 21, 1982), p. B-10.
2. "And Now, Gay Family Rights?," *Time* (Dec. 13, 1982), p. 74. Mayor Diane Feinstein vetoed the ordinance.
3. "All in the Family," *Time* (June 16, 1980), p. 31.
4. *See* Bruce C. Hafen, *The Constitutional Status of Marriage, Kinship, and Sexual Privacy—Balancing the Individual and Social Interests,* 81 Michigan Law Review 463, 464 (1983).
5. *See generally* Kenneth Karst, *The Freedom of Intimate Association,* 89 Yale Law Journal 624 (1980).
6. *People v. Onofre,* 51 N.Y. 2d 476, 488, 415 N.E.2d 936, 940, 434 N.Y.S. 2d 947, 951 (1980), *cert. denied,* 451 U.S. 987 (1981).
7. *In re Adoption of Adult Anonymous,* 106 Misc. 2d 792, 435 N.Y.S. 2d 527 (1981). In another New York county, however, a court disallowed an adoption between adult males because no child-parent relationship would be created. *In re Anonymous II,* 111 Misc. 2d 320, 443 N.Y.S. 2d 1008 (1981).
8. *See Commonwealth v. Bonadio,* 490 Pa. 91, 415 A. 2d 47 (1980).
9. Henry H. Foster, Jr. and Doris Jones Freed, *A Bill of Rights for Children,* 6 Family Law Quarterly 343, 347 (1972).
10. Hafen, *op. cit.,* p. 473.
11. Jeremy Bentham, 1 *Theory of Legislation* (Boston: Weeks, Jordan and Company, 1840), p. 248.
12. *See* John Locke, *The Second Treatise of Government* (Indianapolis: Bobbs-Merrill, 1952).
13. Hafen, *op. cit.,* p. 473.
14. Foster and Freed, *op. cit.,* p. 347.
15. Joseph Goldstein, Anna Freud and Albert J. Solnit, *Beyond the Best Interest of the Child,* 2d ed. (New York: Free Press, 1979), p. 6.
16. *Ibid.,* pp. 31-32.
17. *See generally* Michael Wald, *State Intervention on Behalf of "Neglected" Children: A Search for Realistic Standards,* 27 Stanford Law Review 985 (1975).
18. Robert Nisbet, *Twilight of Authority* (New York: Oxford University Press, 1975), p. 84.
19. *See* Hafen, *op. cit.,* p. 474.
20. Max Rheinstein, *Marriage Stability, Divorce, and the Law* (Chicago: University of Chicago Press, 1972), p. 231.
21. Hafen, *op. cit.,* p. 475.
22. Christopher Lasch, *Haven in a Heartless World: The Famiy Besieged* (New York: Basic Books, 1977), p. 123 (emphasis supplied).
23. *Ibid.,* p. 478.
24. *Ibid.,* p. 186.

25. *Ibid.*, p. 125.
26. Hafen, *op. cit.*, pp. 475-76.
27. Lasch, *op. cit.*, p. 189.
28. Peter L. Berger and Richard John Neuhaus, *To Empower People: The Role of Mediating Structures in Public Policy* (Washington: American Enterprise Institute for Public Policy Research, 1977), p. 3.
29. *Ibid.*, p. 6.
30. *Ibid.*, p. 19.
31. Hafen, *op. cit.*, p. 480.
32. Philip B. Heymann and Douglas E. Barzelay, *The Forest and the Trees: Roe v. Wade and Its Critics*, 53 Boston University Law Review 765, 772 (1973).
33. Allan C. Carlson, "The Decline and Fall of Mom and Apple Pie: America's Curious Turn Toward 'Social Parenting,' 1962-1984," 8 *Persuasion at Work* 1 (Jan. 1985) (emphasis supplied).
34. *See* Margaret Mead, "A Cultural Anthropologist's Approach to Maternal Deprivation," *Deprivation of Maternal Care: A Reassessment of Its Effects* (New York: Schocken Books, 1972), pp. 223-51.
35. Margaret O'Brien Steinfels, *Who's Minding the Children?: The History and Politics of Day Care in America* (New York: Simon and Schuster, 1973), p. 78 (emphasis supplied).
36. Catherine R. Stimpson, *Discrimination Against Women: Congressional Hearing on Equal Rights in Education and Employment* (New York: R. R. Bowker, 1973), p. 542.
37. *Ibid.*
38. As quoted in Carlson, *op. cit.*, p. 4.
39. Bernard Greenblatt, *Responsibility for Child Care: The Changing Role of Family and State in Child Development* (San Francisco: Jossey-Bass, 1977), p. 270.
40. Carlson, *op. cit.*, p. 7.
41. *Ibid. Also see* Dale Mears, "International Day Care: A Selective Review and Psychoanalytic Critique," *Congressional Record* (Dec. 2, 1971), pp. S 44128-34; Hilda Scott, *Sweden's 'Right to Be Human': Sex Role Equality: The Goal and the Reality* (Armonk, N.J.: M. E. Sharpe, 1982), pp. 99-116; "An Eden in Sweden?," *Newsweek* (Sept. 10, 1984), p. 20; and, Edward M. Levine, "Dare Care: Cons, Costs, Kids," *Chicago Tribune* (Sept. 18, 1984), p. 15.
42. "Looking Ahead: Nine Top Women Eye the Future," *Working Women* (Dec. 1982), p. 117.
43. Berger and Neuhaus, *op. cit.*, p. 44.
44. Hafen, *op. cit.*, p. 281 (emphasis supplied).
45. Heymann and Barzelay, *op. cit.*, p. 773.
46. *Ibid.*
47. D. H. Lawrence, *A Propos of Lady Chatterly's Lover* (New York: Haskell House, 1973), pp. 35-36 (emphasis supplied).
48. Hafen, *op. cit.*, p. 481.

Chapter Four

1. *See generally* Steven W. Mosher, *Broken Earth: The Rural Chinese* (New York: Free Press, 1983).
2. *See generally* Samuel Radbill, "Children in a World of Violence: A History of Child Abuse," *The Battered Child* (Chicago: University of Chicago Press, 1983).
3. Mason P. Thomas, Jr., *Child Abuse and Neglect: Historical Overview, Legal Matrix, and Social Perspectives,* 50 North Carolina Law Review 293, 294 (1972).
4. *Ibid.*, p. 295 (footnote omitted).
5. *Ibid.*
6. *Ibid.*
7. *Ibid.*, p. 296.
8. Radbill, *op. cit.*, pp. 5-6.
9. *Ibid.*, p. 4.
10. *See* George Payne, *The Child in Human Progress* (New York: G. P. Putnam's Sons, 1916), pp. 257-71.
11. *Ibid.*, pp. 306-11.
12. Joseph Goldstein, Anna Freud, and Albert J. Solnit, *Beyond the Best Interests of the Child* (New York: Free Press, 1973), p. 13.
13. Patricia K. Naherny and José Rosario, "Morality, Science, and the Use of the Child in History," *Schooling and the Rights of Children,* Vernon F. Haubrich and Michael W. Apple, eds. (Berkeley, Calif.: McCutchan Publishing Corporation, 1975), p. 2.
14. Philippe Ariès, *Centuries of Childhood: A Social History of the Family* (New York: Random House, 1962).
15. *Ibid.*, p. 128.
16. J. H. Plumb, "The Great Change in Children," 13 *Horizon* (Winter 1971), p. 6.
17. *Ibid.*, p. 7.
18. *See* Norbert Elias, *The Civilizing Process: The History of Manners* (New York: Urizen Books, 1978), p. 72.
19. *Ibid.*, p. 69.
20. Neil Postman, *The Disappearance of Childhood* (New York: Delacorte Press, 1982), p. 16.
21. Lloyd deMause, "The Evolution of Childhood," *The History of Childhood,* Lloyd deMause, ed. (New York: The Psychohistory Press, 1974), p. 39.
22. Ariès, *op. cit.*, p. 103.
23. *Ibid.*
24. Naherny and Rosario, *op. cit.*, p. 8.
25. William Barclay, *The Ten Commandments for Today* (Grand Rapids, Mich.: Eerdmans, 1973), pp. 63, 64.

Chapter Five

1. Neil Postman, *The Disappearance of Childhood* (New York: Delacorte Press, 1982), p. 151.

2. John W. Richard, "Carle Zimmerman's Sociology of the Family," 22 *The Mankind Quarterly* Nos. 1 & 2 (Fall and Winter 1982), pp. 55-68.
3. *See, in general,* Carle C. Zimmerman, *Family and Civilization* (New York: Harper and Row, 1947). *Also see* Carle C. Zimmerman and Lucious F. Cervantes, *Marriage and the Family* (Chicago: Henry Regnery, 1956).
4. Henry Sumner Maine, *Ancient Law* (London: John Murray, 1861), p. 126 (emphasis in original).
5. *Ibid.*, p. 168.
6. *Ibid.*
7. Genesis 2:18-24.
8. Genesis 1:28. *See also* Genesis 9:1.
9. Genesis 4:1.
10. Genesis 48:9.
11. Joshua 24:34.
12. Psalms 128:3.
13. Jeremiah 1:1.
14. 2 Corinthians 12:14.
15. 1 Timothy 5:8.
16. 1 Thessalonians 2:7.
17. Matthew 19:13 (emphasis supplied).
18. Matthew 19:14.
19. Matthew 19:15.
20. *See* Luke 9:46-48; Matthew 18:5; Mark 10:15; Luke 18:17.
21. *Ibid.*
22. *See, for example,* 2 Corinthians 12:14; Titus 2:4.
23. Hebrews 11:23.
24. Hebrews 12:9.
25. Hebrews 12:9. *See also* Proverbs 23:13, 14.
26. Ephesians 6:4.
27. Proverbs 22:6.
28. Deuteronomy 6:6, 7.
29. Deuteronomy 4:9.
30. 2 Timothy 3:16, 17.
31. Deuteronomy 33:10.
32. Proverbs 1:7.

Chapter Six

1. Isidore Stan, Lewis Paul Todd, and Merle Curtis, *Living American Documents* (New York: Harcourt, Brace and World, 1961), p. 5.
2. *See generally* Perry Miller, *The New England Mind—The Seventeenth Century* (Cambridge: Harvard University Press, 1954); *The Puritans* (New York: Harper and Row, 1963); *Orthodoxy in Massachusetts, 1630-1650* (New York: Harper and Row, 1970).
3. Willystine Goodsell, *A History of the Family as a Social and Educational Institution* (New York: MacMillan, 1915), p. 353.

4. George Haskins, *Law and Authority in Early Massachusettes* (New York: Macmillan, 1960), p. 80.
5. Edmund Morgan, *The Puritan Family: Religion and Domestic Relations in Seventeenth Century New England* (New York: Harper and Row, 1966), pp. 25-28, 106. *Also see* Arthur Calhoun, *A Social History of the American Family from Colonial Times to the Present* (New York: Arno Press, 1973), Vol. 1, pp. 41, 47, 83; Goodsell, *op. cit.*, p. 353.
6. Haskins, *op. cit.*, p. 80.
7. Calhoun, *op. cit.*, Vol. 1, p. 75.
8. *Ibid.*, p. 51.
9. Morgan, *op. cit.*, pp. 25-28, 106. Goodsell, *op. cit.*, p. 353. Calhoun, *op. cit.*, Vol. 1, pp. 41, 47, 83. *Also see* Susan Tiffin, *In Whose Best Interest* (Westport, Conn.: Greenwood Press, 1982), p. 16.
10. Lawrence Cremin, *American Education: The Colonial Experience, 1607-1783* (New York: Harper and Row, 1970), p. 40. Cremin states that the Bible, throughout the seventeenth century, remained the single most important influence in the lives of Anglo-Americans.
11. Calhoun, *op. cit.*, Vol. 1, pp. 83, 41, 47. On p. 72 Calhoun quotes the Colonial Records of Connecticut (1643) on this point: "The prosperity and well being of Commonwealth doth much depend upon the well government and ordering of particular families, which in an ordinary way cannot be expected when rules of God are neglected in laying the foundation of a family state." *Also see* Morgan, *op. cit.*, pp. 25-28, 106. Tiffin, *op. cit.*, p. 16. Goodsell, *op. cit.*, p. 353.
12. *Ibid.*
13. Cremin, *op. cit.*, p. 50.
14. *Ibid.*, pp. 51, 52.
15. *Ibid.*, p. 51.
16. *Ibid.*, p. 124.
17. Calhoun, *op. cit.*, p. 67.
18. Cremin, *op. cit.*, p. 124.
19. *Ibid.*, p. 135.
20. *Ibid.*, pp. 135, 136.
21. *Ibid.*, p. 128.
22. Morgan, *op. cit.*, pp. 87-108. *See also* Ellwood Cubberly, *The History of Education* (New York: Houghton Mifflin Co., 1920), pp. 374, 360. Calhoun, *op. cit.*, p. 75.
23. Cremin, *op. cit.*, p. 130. The texts used included *The New England Primer* (1690), *The Westminster Catechism* (1647), and John Cotton's *Milk for Babes, Drawn Out of the Breasts of Both Testaments* (1646).
24. *Ibid.*, p. 49.
25. Harvey Wish, *Society and Thought in Early America* (New York: Longmans Green, 1950), p. 55.
26. Calhoun, *op. cit.*, Vol. 1, p. 110.
27. Cremin, *op. cit.*, p. 133.
28. Calhoun, *op. cit.*, p. 124.

29. *See* E. Alice Beshoner, *Home Education in America: Parental Rights Reasserted*, 49 Missouri Law Review 191, 191-192 (1981).
30. *Records of the Governor and Company of Massachusetts Bay in New England,* 1647, Vol. II, p. 203. *See also* Henry Steele Commanger, ed., *Documents of American History* (New York: Appleton-Century-Crofts, Inc., 1949), p. 29.
31. *Ibid.*, p. 203.
32. Cubberly, *op. cit.*, pp. 365, 366. Beshoner, *op. cit.*, pp. 191, 192.
33. Cremin, *op. cit.*, p. 129. *Also see* William T. Davis, *History of the Town of Plymouth* (Philadelphia: J. W. Lewis & Co., 1885), p. 52.
34. Haskins, *op. cit.*, pp. 78-81. Cubberly, *op. cit.*, pp. 365, 374. It was literally a state-church, with the state being a servant of the church.
35. *See* Thomas Barnes, *The Book of the General Lawes and Libertyes Concerning the Inhabitants of the Massachusets* (San Marino, Calif.: The Huntington Library facsimile of the 1648 edition, 1975), p. 6.
36. Haskins, *op. cit.*, p. 79. *See, for example* the preamble or introduction of the General Court to the Inhabitants of Massachusetts in *The Book of the General Lawes and Libertyes Concerning the Inhabitants of the Massachusets* (Cambridge, 1648), p. A-2.
37. *Ibid.*, p. 81.
38. Calhoun, *op. cit.*, p. 71.
39. Goodsell, *op. cit.*, p. 396.
40. Haskins, *op. cit.*, p. 81. Calhoun, *op. cit.*, p. 119.
41. Calhoun, *op. cit.*, p. 119. Goodsell, *op. cit.*, p. 400.
42. As quoted in Calhoun, *op. cit.*, p. 119.
43. *The Book of the General Lawes and Libertyes Concerning the Inhabitants of the Massachusets* (Cambridge, 1648), p. 6.
44. Haskins, *op. cit.*, p. 81. Calhoun, *op. cit.*, p. 121.
45. *The Book of the General Lawes and Libertyes Concerning the Inhabitants of the Massachusets* (Cambridge, 1648), p. 6.
46. Calhoun, *op. cit.*, p. 77. Haskins, *op. cit.*, p. 81.
47. Calhoun, *op. cit.*, p. 77.
48. *Ibid.*, p. 120.
49. *The Book of the General Lawes and Libertyes Concerning the Inhabitants of the Massachusets* (Cambridge, 1648), p. 12.
50. Cremin, *op. cit.*, p. 119. Calhoun, *op. cit.*, p. 74.
51. *Records of the Governor and Company of Massachusetts Bay in New England,* 1642 (June 14), pp. 6, 7.
52. *The Book of the General Lawes and Libertyes Concerning the Inhabitants of the Massachusets* (Cambridge, 1648), p. 11. These laws also had the disturbing feature that in cases of continual neglect of such requirements, and where the child remains "rude, stubborn and unruly," the child could be removed from his parents and placed with someone who would carry out the law, or "apprenticed" into another household. *Ibid.*
53. *Ibid.* Children were to be able to answer the questions propounded to

them from the catechism by parents or select-men. Parents were also required to teach their children some lawful calling under the statute. *Ibid.*

54. Cremin, *op. cit.*, p. 124.
55. *Ibid.*, p. 119. Similarly, in England, King Henry VIII ordered parsons and vicars to admonish parents to "teach children regarding the Christian faith." *Ibid.*
56. *Ibid.*, p. 125.
57. *Ibid.*
58. Calhoun, *op. cit.*, p. 74.
59. Cremin, *op. cit.*, p. 125.
60. Beshoner, *op. cit.*, p. 191.
61. John Miller, *The First Frontier: Life in Colonial America* (New York: Delacorte Press, 1966), pp. 224, 225. The same was also true in the southern colonies. Cremin, *op. cit.*, pp. 135, 136. *Also see* Calhoun, *op. cit.*, pp. 229-244.
62. Calhoun, *op. cit.*, p. 75.
63. Lawrence Kotin and William Aikman, *Legal Foundations of Compulsory School Attendance* (Port Washington, N.Y.: Keninkat Press, 1980), p. 20.
64. *Ibid.*, pp. 20, 21.
65. Newton Edwards and Herman Richey, *The School in the American Social Order* (Boston: Houghton-Mifflin Co., 1947), pp. 108, 109. Other reasons suggested are the impracticalities of enforcement in frontier America, and the social breakdown due to the Indian wars. Kotin and Aikman, *op. cit.*, pp. 22, 23.
66. Edwards and Richey, *op. cit.*, pp. 108, 109; Kotin and Aikman, *op. cit.*, p. 23.
67. Kotin and Aikman, *op. cit.*, pp. 20, 21.

Chapter Seven

1. Willystine Goodsell, *A History of the Family as a Social and Educational Institution* (New York: Macmillan, 1915), p. 353; Cremin, *American Education: The Colonial Experience, 1607-1783* (New York: Harper and Row, 1970), pp. 479-485.
2. Arthur Calhoun, *A Social History of the American Family from Colonial Times to the Present* (New York: Arno Press, 1973), Vol. II, pp. 54, 138; Lawrence Cremin, *American Education: The Colonial Experience, 1607-1783* (New York: Harper and Row, 1970), pp. 479-485.
3. Calhoun, *op. cit.*, Vol III, pp. 229-244.
4. Cremin, *op. cit.*, pp. 124, 479-485.
5. *Ibid.*, pp. 479-485, 411.
6. Calhoun, *op. cit.*, Vol. II, p. 11.
7. *Ibid.*
8. Cremin, *op. cit.*, pp. 480, 481.
9. *Ibid.*, p. 113.
10. *Ibid.*, p. 135.

11. *Ibid.*, pp. 479-485, 113, 124-129, 135; Lawrence Cremin, *The American Common School* (New York: Columbia University, 1951), pp. 87, 88.
12. Cremin, *The American Common School, op. cit.*, pp. 87, 88.
13. *Ibid.*, p. 88.
14. Cremin, *American Education: The Colonial Experience, 1607-1783, op. cit.*, pp. 479-485, 113, 124-129, 135. *Also see* John W. Whitehead and Wendell R. Bird, *Home Education and Constitutional Liberties* (Westchester, Ill.: Crossway Books, 1984), pp. 22-25.
15. John C. Fitzpatrick, *George Washington Himself* Indianapolis: Bobbs-Merrill Co., 1933), p. 19. *See* especially William H. Wilbur, *The Making of George Washington,* 2d ed. (Daytona Beach: Patriotic Education Inc., 1973).
16. Cremin, *American Education: The Colonial Experience, 1607-1783, op. cit.*, p. 483.
17. Robert Douthat Meade, *Patrick Henry: Patriot in the Making* (Philadelphia: J. B. Lippincott, 1957), p. 5.
18. Ian Elliot, ed., *James Madison 1751-1836* (New York: Oceana, 1969), p. 1.
19. John Bigelow, *The Life of Benjamin Franklin, Written by Himself* (Philadelphia: J. B. Lippincott, 1916), Vol. I, p. 99.
20. John C. Fitzpatrick, ed., *The Writings of George Washington* (Washington, D.C.: United States Government Printing Office, 1932), Vol. III, p. 130.
21. Cremin, *American Education: The Colonial Experience, 1607-1783, op. cit.*, p. 486.
22. *Diary of Cotton Mather* (New York: Frederick Ungar Pub. Co., 1957), Vol. I, pp. 534-537.
23. Cremin, *American Education: The Colonial Experience, 1607-1783, op. cit.*, p. 483.
24. *Ibid.*
25. *Ibid.*, pp. 479, 549, 550.
26. *Ibid.*
27. James Tobak and Perry Zirkel, *Home Instruction: An Analysis of the Statutes and Case Law,* 8 University of Dayton Law Review 13, 14 (1982).
28. Cremin, *American Education: The Colonial Experience, 1607-1783, op. cit.*, pp. 549, 550.
29. *Ibid.*, p. 550.
30. *Ibid.*, p. 543.
31. Pierre Samuel Dupont de Nemoirs, *National Education in the United States of America* (Newark, Del.: Univ. of Delaware Press, 1923), pp. 3, 4. *Also see* Cremin, *op. cit.*, p. 543.
32. Cremin, *op. cit.*, p. 550.
33. Charles Adams, ed., III *The Works of John Adams* (Boston, 1851), pp. 456, 452.
34. *Ibid.*

35. Cremin, *op. cit.*, p. 267.
36. Saul K. Padover, *Jefferson* (New York: Harcourt-Brace, 1942), p. 369.
37. Cremin, *op. cit.*, pp. 442, 440; Murray Rothbard, *Education: Free and Compulsory* (Wichita, Kan.: Center for Independent Education, 1977), pp. 42-44. In fact, Jefferson proposed "free" school for those who were unable to receive a proper education elsewhere. *Id.*
38. Cremin, *op. cit.*, pp. 277, 278.
39. James Axtell, ed., *The Educational Writings of John Locke* (Cambridge: Cambridge University Press, 1968), pp. 241, 260, 153-159, 313, 314.
40. *Ibid.*
41. Cremin, *op. cit.*, p. 301.
42. *Ibid.*, p. 466.
43. *The Works of the Rev. John Witherspoon,* 2d ed. (Philadelphia: William Woodard, 1802), Vol. IV, p. 133.
44. Calhoun, *op. cit.*, pp. 57, 58.
45. Ord. of 1787, July 13, 1787, Art. 3, reprinted in *Documents Illustrative of the Formation of the Union of American States* (Washington, D.C.: United States Government Printing Office, 1927), p. 52.
46. *See* Howard Cohen, *Equal Rights for Children* (Totowa, N.J.: Rowman and Littlefield, 1980), pp. 5-7, for a discussion of John Locke's views on children and parents.
47. John Locke, *Second Treatise of Government* (Indianapolis: Bobbs-Merrill, 1952), p. 33.

Chapter Eight

1. John C. H. Wu, *Fountain of Justice* (Beaverton, Ore.: International Scholarly Book Services, 1980), p. 65.
2. Bruce C. Hafen, *Children's Liberation and the New Egalitarianism: Some Reservations About Abandoning Youth to Their Rights,* 1976 Brigham Young Law Review 605, 615.
3. *Ibid.*
4. *See, for example,* Harriet Philpel, *Minor's Rights to Medical Care,* 36 Albany Law Review 462 (1972).
5. *See Poe v. Gerstein,* 517 F.2d 787, 789 (5th Cir. 1975), for a contrary view.
6. *In re Hudson,* 13 Wash. 2d 673, 685, 126 P.2d 765, 771 (1942).
7. *People ex rel. Portnoy v. Strasser,* 303 N.Y. 539, 542, 104 N.E.2d 895, 896 (1952).
8. *Lacher v. Venus,* 177 Wis. 558, 569-70, 188 N.W. 613, 617 (1922).
9. *Commonwealth v. Armstrong,* 1 Pa. L. J. Rep. 393 (1842).
10. *Ibid.*, pp. 393-95 (emphasis in original).
11. *Ibid.*, pp. 395-96 (emphasis in original).
12. *Ibid.*, pp. 396-97.
13. *Ibid.*, pp. 397-98 (emphasis and capitalization in original).
14. *Ibid.*, p. 398.
15. *Ibid.*

16. William Mack, ed., 29 *Cyclopedia of Law and Procedure* (New York: American Law Book Co., 1908), p. 1548. Other older cases upholding parental rights include: *Denton v. James*, 107 Kan. 729, 193 P.307 (1920); *Hardivich v. Board of School Trustees*, 54 Cal. 696, 205 P.49 (1921); *Norval v. Zinmaster*, 57 Neb. 158, 77 N.W. 373 (1898); *State ex rel. Kelly v. Ferguson*, 144 N.W. 1039 (Neb. 1914); *People v. Turner*, 55 Ill. 280 (1870); *Stapleton v. Poynter*, 111 Kentucky 264 (1901); *Jamison v. Gilbert*, 135 P.342 (Okl. 1913); *Rulison v. Post*, 79 Ill. 567 (1875); *Lacker v. Venus*, 188 N.W. 613 (Wis. 1922); *Commonwealth v. Roberts*, 159 Mass. 372 (1893); *State v. Peterman*, 32 Ind. App. 665, 70 N.E. 550 (1904); *Board of Education v. Purse*, 101 Ga. 422 (1897); *Roller v. Roller*, 37 Wash. 242 (1905); *Tremain's Case*, 1 Strange 167 (1719).
17. Hafen, *op. cit.*, p. 616.
18. Philip B. Heymann and Douglas E. Barzelay, *The Forest and the Trees: Roe v. Wade and Its Critics*, 53 Boston University Law Review 765, 772-73 (1973) (emphasis supplied).
19. Hafen, *op. cit.*, p. 617.
20. *Matarese v. Matarese*, 17 R.I. 131, 132-133, 131 A.198, 199 (1925) (emphasis supplied).
21. *In re Guardianship of Faust*, 239 Miss. 299, 305-07, 123 So.2d 218, 220-21 (1960) (emphasis supplied).
22. Perry Miller, *The Life of the Mind in America* (London: Victor Gallancz, 1966), p. 115.
23. Daniel Boorstin, *The Mysterious Science of the Law* (Mangolia, Mass.: Peter Smith, 1958), p. 3.
24. William Blackstone, *Commentaries on the Laws of England*, Vol. 2, George Tucker, ed. (Philadelphia: William Birch Young and Abraham Small, 1803), p. 452 (emphasis supplied).
25. *In re Agar-Ellis*, 24 Ch. D. 317 (C.A.) (1883).
26. Hafen, *op. cit.*, p. 618.

Chapter Nine

1. Comment, *Ajudicating What Yoder Left Unresolved: Religious Rights for Minor Children After Danforth and Carey*, 126 Pennsylvania Law Review 1135, 1143 (1978).
2. 262 U.S. 390.
3. *Id.* at 399.
4. *Id.* at 400.
5. *Id.* at 401-02.
6. *Id.* at 402.
7. 268 U.S. 510 (1925).
8. *Id.* at 535.
9. 390 U.S. 629 (1968).
10. *Id.* at 639.
11. *Id.* at 640 (emphasis supplied).
12. 405 U.S. 645 (1972).

13. *Id.* at 651.
14. *See May v. Anderson,* 345 U.S. 528, 533 (1953).
15. 381 U.S. 479 (1965).
16. 410 U.S. 113 (1973).
17. 381 U.S. at 495 (emphasis supplied).
18. 406 U.S. 205 (1972).
19. *Id.* at 230 (emphasis supplied).
20. *Id.* at 232.
21. 431 U.S. 494 (1977).
22. *Id.* at 504.
23. *Id.* at 503 (emphasis supplied).
24. 431 U.S. 816 (1977).
25. *Id.* at 846-47.
26. *Id.* at 845.
27. *Id.*
28. 455 U.S. 743 (1982).
29. *Id.* at 769.
30. *Id.* at 759-760.
31. *Id.*
32. *Id.* at 766-767.
33. *Id.* at 753-754.
34. *Id.* at 754-755 (emphasis supplied).
35. Bruce C. Hafen, *Children's Liberation and the New Egalitarianism: Some Reservations About Abandoning Youth to Their Rights,* 1976 Brigham Young Law Review 605, 626.
36. 262 U.S. at 399.
37. 405 U.S. at 651.
38. Hafen, *op. cit.,* p. 627.
39. *Mattis v. Schnan,* 502 F.2d 588 (8th Cir. 1974).
40. *Id.* at 595 (emphasis supplied).

Chapter Ten

1. James Tobak and Perry Zirkel, *Home Instruction: An Analysis of the Statutes and Case Law,* 8 University of Dayton Law Review 13, 14 (1982).
2. *Ibid.*
3. *See generally* Samuel L. Blumenfeld, *Is Public Education Necessary?* (Old Greenwich, Conn.: Devon-Adair, 1981).
4. *See* John W. Whitehead and Wendell R. Bird, *Home Education and Constitutional Liberties* (Westchester, Ill.: Crossway Books, 1984), pp. 13-18.
5. As cited in "Another Study Says Schools Are in Peril," *Washington Post* (July 20, 1983), p. A-2.
6. William V. Shannon, "Too Much, Too Soon," *New York Times* (September 8, 1976), p. 37 (emphasis supplied).
7. *See* John W. Whitehead, *The Stealing of America* (Westchester, Ill.: Crossway Books, 1982), pp. 85-90.

8. *See McCollum v. Board of Education,* 333 U.S. 203 (1948).
9. *See, for example, Engel v. Vitale,* 370 U.S. 421 (1962); *School District of Abington Township, Pa. v. Schempp,* 374 U.S. 203 (1962).
10. These hearings were held on the proposed regulations for the Protection of Pupil Rights Amendment which is informally known as the Hatch Amendment.
11. Phyllis Schlafly, ed., *Child Abuse in the Classroom* (Westchester, Ill.: Crossway Books, 1985), p. 39.
12. *Ibid.*, pp. 39, 40.
13. *Ibid.*, p. 40.
14. *Ibid.*, pp. 40, 41.
15. *Ibid.*, p. 41.
16. *Ibid.*, pp. 56, 57.
17. *Ibid.*, p. 57.
18. *Exparte Crouse,* 4 Whart. 9 (Pa. 1839).
19. *Id.* at 11. *Also see Milwaukee Industrial School v. Supervisors of Milwaukee County,* 40 Wis. 328, 330 (1876).
20. Mason P. Thomas, Jr., *Child Abuse and Neglect: Historical Overview,* Legal Matrix, and Social Perspectives, 50 North Carolina Law Review 293, 307-09 (1972).
21. Act of April 21, 1899, § 21, [1899] Ill. Laws 137.
22. *Id.* at 133.
23. Thomas, *op. cit.*, p. 326.
24. *Ibid.*, p. 331.
25. 387 U.S. 1 (1967).
26. *Id.* at 13.
27. 393 U.S. 503 (1969).
28. *Id.* at 511.
29. *Id.* at 515.
30. *Id.* at 518, 522.
31. 419 U.S. 565 (1975).
32. *Id.* at 576.
33. *Id.* at 590-91 (emphasis in original).
34. 53 U.S.L.W. 4083 (January 15, 1985).
35. *Id.* at 4086.

Chapter Eleven

1. 125 U.S. 190 (1888)
2. *Id.* at 210-211.
3. 262 U.S. 390 (1923).
4. 431 U.S. 494 (1977).
5. 381 U.S. 479 (1965).
6. 405 U.S. 438 (1972).
7. Peter J. Riga, *The Supreme Court's View of Marriage and the Family: Tradition or Transition?,* 18 Journal of Family Law 301, 203-03 (1979-80).
8. 410 U.S. 113 (1973).

9. Riga, *op. cit.*, p. 304.
10. 410 U.S. at 153.
11. *Id.*
12. *Id.* (emphasis supplied).
13. To those who would challenge this conclusion, I would refer them to the annual average of one million plus abortions performed in the United States since the decision in *Roe* in 1973 as well as Justice White's dissent in *Planned Parenthood v. Danforth*, 428 U.S. 52, 92 (1976): "In *Roe v. Wade* . . . this Court recognized a right to an abortion free from state prohibition."
14. 428 U.S. 52 (1976).
15. *Id.* at 69, 71.
16. *Id.* at 70 (emphasis supplied).
17. *Id.* at 73.
18. *Id.* at 75.
19. *Id.* In the companion case to *Danforth, Bellotti v. Baird,* 428 U.S. 132 (1976), the Court found unconstitutional a state law requiring parental written consent before an abortion could be performed on an unmarried minor, but providing that an abortion could be obtained under court order upon a showing of good cause if one or both parents refused consent. In *Bellotti II,* 442 U.S. 622 (1979), the Court reaffirmed the unconstitutionality of the statute involved in *Bellotti I* but with some language favorable to the parents' role in the upbringing of children. *Id.* at 633-39.
20. George Gilder, *Sexual Suicide* (New York: Quadrangle Books, 1973), p. 15.
21. Alvin Toffler, *The Third Wave* (New York: Bantam Books, 1980), p. 215.
22. Spencer Rich, "One-Parent Families Found to Increase Sharply in U.S.," *Washington Post* (May 15, 1985), p. A-17.
23. 431 U.S. 678 (1977).
24. *Doe v. Irwin,* 428 F. Supp. 1198 (W.D. Mich. 1977), vacated without opinion, 599 F.2d 1219 (6th Cir. 1977).
25. 450 U.S. 398 (1981).
26. 428 U.S. at 64.
27. Bruce C. Hafen, *Puberty, Privacy, and Protection,* 63 American Bar Association Law Journal 1383, 1386 (October 1977) (emphasis supplied).
28. *Id.* at 1388.
29. Comment, *Adjudicating What Yoder Left Unresolved: Religious Rights for Minor Children After Danforth and Carey,* 126 University of Pennsylvania Law Review 1125, 1155 (1977).
30. *Id.*
31. *Id.* at 1159 (footnote omitted).
32. Riga, *op. cit.*, pp. 304-05.
33. 406 U.S. 205, 242 (1972) (emphasis supplied).
34. Comment, *op. cit.*, pp. 1152-53.

35. 13 Misc. 2d 318, 178 N.Y.S. 2d 328 (Sup. Ct. 1958).
36. *Id.* at 321, 178 N.Y.S. 2d at 331.
37. *Id.*
38. Laurence Tribe, *Childhood, Suspect Classifications, and Conclusive Presumptions: Three Linked Riddles*, 39 Law and Contemporary Problems 8, 35 (1975).
39. 428 U.S. at 73.
40. *Bellotti v. Baird*, 443 U.S. 622, 638 (1979).
41. 450 U.S. at 410.
42. 1980 Lecture at *American Family Institute* (Washington, D.C.) (emphasis in original).

Chapter Twelve

1. *See* Bruce C. Hafen, *Children's Liberation and the New Egalitarianism: Some Reservations About Abandoning Youth to Their "Rights,"* 1976 Brigham Young Law Review 605, 644.
2. *Ibid.*
3. *Ibid.*, p. 646.
4. *Ibid.*, p. 648 (emphasis supplied).
5. *Oregon v. Mitchell*, 400 U.S. 112, 240 (1970) (Brennan, White, Marshall, JJ., concurring).
6. U.S. Const. Art. I, §§ 2, 3; Art, II, § 1.
7. Hafen, *op. cit.*, p. 647.
8. *Ibid.*, p. 648.
9. David A. J. Richards, *The Individual, the Family, and the Constitution: A Jurisprudential Perspective*, 55 New York University Law Review 1, 28 (1980) (emphasis supplied).
10. *Ibid.*
11. *Ibid.*
12. Richard Farson, *Birthrights* (New York: Macmillan, 1974).
13. *Ibid.*, p. 27.
14. *Ibid.*
15. *Ibid.*
16. *Ibid.*
17. *Ibid.*, p. 31 (emphasis supplied).
18. *Ibid.*, p. 41.
19. *Ibid.*
20. *Ibid.*, p. 43.
21. *Ibid.*
22. *Ibid.*, pp. 47, 48 (emphasis supplied).
23. *Ibid.*, p. 43.
24. *Ibid.*, p. 70.
25. *Ibid.*
26. *Ibid.*, p. 78.
27. *Ibid.*, p. 77 (emphasis supplied).
28. *Ibid.*, p. 85.
29. *Ibid.*, p. 86.

30. *Ibid.*, p. 87.
31. The United States Congress has addressed this problem in the Hatch Amendment, which provides parental access to public school records on their children. *See* 20 U.S.C. 1232(h).
32. Farson, *op. cit.*, p. 98 (footnote omitted).
33. *Ibid.*, p. 107.
34. *Ibid.*, p. 108.
35. *Ibid.*, p. 109.
36. *Ibid.*, p. 111.
37. *See generally Wisconsin v. Yoder,* 406 U.S. 205 (1972).
38. Farson, *op. cit.*, p. 121 (emphasis supplied).
39. *See Ingraham v. Wright,* 430 U.S. 651 (1977).
40. Farson, *op. cit.*, pp. 116, 117.
41. *Ibid.*, p. 130 (emphasis supplied).
42. *Ibid.*, p. 135 (emphasis supplied).
43. *Ibid.*
44. *Ibid.*, pp. 141, 142.
45. *Ibid.*, pp. 146, 147.
46. *Ibid.*, p. 148 (footnote omitted).
47. *Ibid.*, p. 146.
48. *Ibid.*, p. 154.
49. *Ibid.*, p. 184.
50. *Ibid.*, p. 185.
51. Hafen, *op. cit.*, p. 651.
52. *Ibid.*
53. Joseph Goldstein, Anna Freud and Albert J. Solnit, *Beyond the Best Interest of the Child* (New York: Free Press, 1973), pp. 6, 7, 8.
54. Hafen, *op. cit.*, p. 651.

Chapter Thirteen

1. *See* Urie Bronfenbrenner, *Two Worlds of Childhood: U.S. and U.S.S.R.* (New York: Russell Sage Foundation, 1970), p. 95.
2. *Ibid.* (emphasis supplied).
3. *Ibid.*, p. 96.
4. *Ibid.*, pp. 96, 97.
5. *Ibid.*, p. 97.
6. *Ibid.*, p. 98.
7. Urie Bronfenbrenner, "Socialization and Social Class Through Time and Space," in Eleanor E. Maccoby, Theodore M. Newcomb, and Eugene L. Hartley, eds., *Reading in Social Psychology* (New York: Holt, Rinehart and Winston, 1958), pp. 400-425.
8. *Ibid.*, p. 424.
9. Bronfenbrenner, *Two Worlds of Childhood, op. cit.*, p. 98 (emphasis supplied).
10. *Ibid.*, p. 99.
11. *Ibid.*

12. Alvin Toffler, *The Third Wave* (New York: William Morrow, 1980), p. 45.
13. *Ibid.*
14. *Ibid.*, p. 81.
15. James Coleman, *The Adolescent Society* (New York: Free Press of Glencoe, 1961), p. 3 (emphasis in original).
16. Havy C. Bredemeier and Richard M. Stephenson, *The Analysis of Social Systems* (New York: Holt, Rinehart, and Winston, 1962), p. 119.
17. Elizabeth Hurlock, *Child Development* (New York: McGraw-Hill, 1942), p. 359.
18. Bronfenbrenner, *Two Worlds of Childhood, op. cit.*, p. 101.
19. *Ibid.*
20. *Ibid.*
21. *Ibid.*, p. 102 (emphasis, in part, supplied).
22. Urie Bronfenbrenner, "The Roots of Alienation," *Influences on Human Development*, Urie Bronfenbrenner, ed. (Hinsdale, Ill.: Dryden Press, 1975), p. 664.
23. *Ibid.*
24. *See* John W. Whitehead, *The Stealing of America* (Westchester, Ill.: Crossway Books, 1983), pp. 60-67.
25. Rousas John Rushdoony, "The Trustee Family and Economics," 9 *The Journal of Christian Reconstruction* 204 (1982-1983).

Chapter Fourteen

1. *Family Law Reporter*, 201:0069-70 (Reference File—Uniform and Model Acts).
2. *Ibid.*, 201—0077-79.
3. *Ibid.*
4. *See* John W. Whitehead, *The Stealing of America* (Westchester, Ill.: Crossway Books, 1983), pp. 115-119.

SELECT BIBLIOGRAPHY

As the heading suggests, the following list of books and articles is not intended as a complete bibliographical guide to the complex and multidimensional subject covered in this book. Rather, it is an alphabetical listing of works primarily relied upon, as well as other works which are related in some way to the topics covered.

Adams, Charles, ed., III. *The Works of John Adams*. Boston, 1851.

"All in the Family." *Time*. June 16, 1980.

"And Now, Gay Family Rights." *Time*. December 13, 1982.

"An Eden in Sweden." *Newsweek*. September 10, 1984.

"Another Study Says Schools Are in Peril." *Washington Post*. July 20, 1983.

Areen, Judith. "Intervention Between Parent and Child: A Reappraisal of the State's Role in Child Neglect and Abuse Cases." *Georgetown Law Journal* 63 (1975), 887.

Ariès, Philippe. *Centuries of Childhood: A Social History of the Family*. New York: Random House, 1962.

Attorney General's Task Force on Family Violence. September 1984.

Axtell, James, ed. *The Educational Writings of John Locke*. Cambridge: Cambridge University Press, 1968.

Barclay, William. *The Ten Commandments for Today*. Grand Rapids, Mich.: Eerdmans, 1973.

Barnes, Thomas G., ed. *The Book of the General Lawes and Libertyes Concerning the Inhabitants of the Massachusets*. San Marino, Calif.: The Huntington Library, 1975.

Bell, Deborah. "Termination of Parental Rights: Recent Judicial and Legislative Trends." *Emory Law Journal* 30 (1981), 1065.

Bentham, Jeremy. *Theory of Legislation*. Vol. 1. Boston: Weeks, Jordan & Co., 1840.

Berger, Peter L. and Neuhaus, Richard John. *To Empower People: The Role of Mediating Structures in Public Policy.* Washington: American Institute for Public Policy Research, 1977.

Beshoner, Alice E. "Home Education in America: Parental Rights Reasserted." *Missouri Law Review* 49 (1981), 191.

Bigelow, John. *The Life of Benjamin Franklin, Written by Himself.* Philadelphia: J. B. Lippincott, 1916.

Blackstone, Sir William. *Blackstone's Commentaries.* 5 vols. Philadelphia: William Birch Young & Abraham Small, 1803.

Blumenfeld, Samuel L. *Is Public Education Necessary?* Old Greenwich, Conn.: Devon-Adair, 1981.

The Book of the General Lawes and Libertyes Concerning the Inhabitants of the Massachusets. Cambridge, 1648.

Boorstin, Daniel. *The Mysterious Science of the Law.* Magnolia, Mass.: Peter Smith, 1958.

Bredemeier, Havy C. and Stephenson, Richard M. *The Analysis of Social Systems.* New York: Holt, Rinehart, and Winston, 1962.

Bronfenbrenner, Urie. "The Roots of Alienation." *Influences on Human Development.* Hinsdale, Ill.: Dryden Press, 1975.

———. "Socialization and Social Class Through Time and Space." *Readings in Social Psychology.* New York: Holt, Rinehart, and Winston, 1958.

———. *Two Worlds of Childhood: U.S. and U.S.S.R.* New York: Russell Sage Foundation, 1970.

Burt, Robert A. "Forcing Protection on Children and Their Parents: The Impact of *Wyman v. James.*" *Michigan Law Revew* 69 (1971), 1259.

Butler, Katherine A. "A Chance to be Heard: An Application of *Bellotti v. Baird* to the Civil Commitment of Minors." *Hastings Law Journal* 32 (1981), 1285.

Calhoun, Arthur. *A Social History of the American Family from Colonial Times to the Present.* Vols. 1-3. New York: Arno Press, 1973.

Carlson, Allan C. "The Decline and Fall of Mom and Apple Pie: America's Curious Turn Toward 'Social Parenting,' 1962-1984." *Persuasion at Work* 8 (Jan. 1985), 1.

Child Abuse and You. Childhelp U.S.A., Woodland Hills, Calif. 91370.

Cohen, Howard. *Equal Rights for Children.* Totowa, N.J.: Rowman and Littlefield, 1980.

Colby, Kimberlee Wood. "When the Family Does Not Pray Together: Religious Rights Within the Family." *Harvard Journal of Law and Public Policy* 5 (1982), 39.

Coleman, James. *The Adolescent Society.* New York: Free Press of Glencoe, 1961.

Collins, Glenn. "Debate Over Rights of Children Is Intensifying." *New York Times,* July 21, 1981.

Commanger, Henry Steele, ed. *Documents of American History.* New York: Appleton-Century-Crofts, Inc., 1949.

Comment. "Adjudicating What Yoder Left Unresolved: Religious Rights for Minor Children After *Danforth* and *Carey*." *Pennsylvania Law Review* 126 (1978), 1135.

Comment. "The Child's Right to 'Life, Liberty, and the Pursuit of Happiness': Suits by Children Against Parents for Abuse, Neglect, and Abandonment." *Rutgers Law Review* 34 (1981), 154.

Comment. "State Intrusion into Family Affairs: Justifications and Limitations." *Stanford Law Review* 26 (1974), 1383.

The Compact Edition of the Oxford English Dictionary. Vol. 1. Oxford: Oxford University Press, 1971.

Cremin, Lawrence. *American Education: The Colonial Experience, 1607-1783*. New York: Harper and Row, 1970.

———. *The American Common School*. New York: Columbia University, 1951.

Cubberly, Ellwood. *The History of Education*. New York: Houghton-Mifflin, 1920.

Davis, William T. *History of the Town of Plymouth*. Philadelphia: J. W. Lewis & Co., 1885.

De Francis, Vincent. *Child Abuse—Preview of a Nationwide Survey*. Denver: American Humane Assoc., 1963.

deMause, Lloyd. "The Evolution of Childhood." *The History of Childhood*. Lloyd deMause, ed. New York: The Psychohistory Press, 1974.

Documents Illustrative of the Formation of the Union of American States. Washington: Government Printing Office, 1927.

Diary of Cotton Mather. New York: Frederick Ungar Pub. Co., 1957.

Dupont, Pierre Samuel de Nemoirs. *National Education in the United States of America*. Newark, Del.: University of Delaware Press, 1923.

Edwards, Newton and Richey, Herman G. *The School in the American Social Order*. Boston: Houghlin-Mufflin, 1963.

Elias, Norbert. *The Civilizing Process: The History of Manners*. New York: Urizen Books, 1978.

Elliot, Ian, ed. *James Madison 1751-1836*. New York: Ocean, 1969.

Farson, Richard. *Birthrights*. New York: Macmillan, 1974.

Fitzpatrick, John C. *George Washington Himself*. Indianapolis: Bobbs-Merrill Co., 1933.

———, ed. *The Writings of George Washington*. Washington, D.C.: U.S. Government Printing Office, 1932.

Foster, Henry H. and Freed, Doris Jones. "A Bill of Rights for Children." *Family Law Quarterly* 6 (1972), 343.

Garvey, John H. "Children and the First Amendment." *Texas Law Review* 57 (1979), 321.

Gest, Ted. "The Other Victims of Child Abuse." *U.S. News and World Report,* April 1, 1985.

Gilder, George. *Sexual Suicide*. New York: Quadrangle Books, 1973.

Goldstein, Joseph, Freud, Anna and Solnet, Albert J. *Beyond the Best Interests of the Child*. 2d ed. New York: Free Press, 1979.

Goodsell, Willystine. *A History of the Family as a Social and Educational Institution*. New York: Macmillan, 1915.

Greenblatt, Bernard. *Responsibility for Child Care: The Changing Role of Family and State in Child Development*. San Francisco: Jossey-Bass, 1977.

Haas, Al. "The New Victims of Child Abuse." *The Philadelphia Inquirer*, June 9, 1985.

Hafen, Bruce C. "Children's Liberation and the New Egalitarianism: Some Reservations About Abandoning Youth to Their Rights." *Brigham Young Law Review* (1976), 605.

———. "The Constitutional Status of Marriage, Kinship, and Sexual Privacy—Balancing the Individual and the Social Interests." *Michigan Law Review* 81 (1983), 463.

———. "Puberty, Privacy, and Protection." *American Bar Association Law Journal* 63 (1977), 1383.

Haskins, George. *Law and Authority in Early Massachusetts*. New York: Macmillan, 1960.

Heymann, Philip B. and Barzelay, Douglas E. "The Forest and the Trees: *Roe v. Wade* and Its Critics." *Boston University Law Review* 53 (1973), 765.

Hurlock, Elizabeth. *Child Development*. New York: McGraw-Hill, 1942.

Karst, Kenneth. "The Freedom of Intimate Association." *Yale Law Journal* 89 (1980), 624.

Kasun, Jacqueline. "Turning Children into Sex Experts." *The Public Interest* 55 (1979), 3.

Keiter, Robert B. "Privacy, Children, and Their Parents: Reflections On and Beyond the Supreme Court's Approach." *Minnesota Law Review* 66 (1982), 459.

Kleinfield, Andrew Jay. "The Balance of Power Among Infants, Their Parents and the State." *Family Law Quarterly* 4 (1970), 410.

Klotin, Lawrence and Aikman, William F. *Legal Foundation of Compulsory School Attendance*. Port Washington, N.Y.: Kennikat Press, 1980.

Lasch, Christopher. *Haven in a Heartless World: The Family Besieged*. New York: Basic Books, 1977.

Lawrence, D. H. *A Propos of Lady Chatterly's Lover*. New York: Haskell House, 1973.

Levine, Edward M. "Day Care: Cons, Costs, Kids." *Chicago Tribune*, September 18, 1984.

Locke, John. *The Second Treatise of Government*. Indianapolis: Bobbs-Merrill, 1952.

"Looking Ahead: Nine Top Women Eye the Future." *Working Women*, December 1982.

Mack, William, editor. *Cyclopedia of Law and Procedure*. New York: American Law Book Co., 1908, Vol. 29.

Maine, Henry Sumner. *Ancient Law*. London: John Murray, 1861.

McCoid, Allan H. "The Battered Child and Other Assaults Upon the Family." *Minnesota Law Review* 50 (1966), 1.

McGinnis, Ronald L. "Sing A Song of Students' Rights." *NOLPE School Law Journal* 6 (1976), 8.

Mead, Margaret. "A Cultural Anthropologist's Approach to Maternal Deprivation." *Deprivation of Maternal Care: A Reassessment of Its Effects*. New York: Schocken Books, 1972.

Meade, Robert D. *Patrick Henry: Patriot in the Making*. Philadelphia: J. B. Lippincott, 1957.

Mears, Dale. "International Day Care: A Selective Review and Psychoanalytic Critique." *Congressional Record*, December 2, 1971.

Miller, John. *The First Frontier: Life in Colonial America*. New York: Delacorte Press, 1966.

Miller, Perry. *The Life of the Mind in America*. London: Victor Gallancz, 1966.

———. *The New England Mind—The Seventeenth Century*. Cambridge: Harvard University Press, 1954.

———. *The Puritans*. New York: Harper and Row, 1963.

———. *Orthodoxy in Massachusetts, 1630-1650*. New York: Harper and Row, 1970.

Morgan, Edmund. *The Puritan Family: Religion and Domestic Relations in Seventeenth Century New England*. New York: Harper and Row, 1966.

Mosher, Steven W. *Broken Earth: The Rural Chinese*. New York: Free Press, 1983.

Naherny, Patricia K. and Rosario, José. "Morality, Science, and the Use of the Child in History." *Schooling and the Rights of Children*. Vernon F. Haubrich and Michael W. Apple, eds. Berkeley, Calif.: McCutchan Publishing Corp., 1975.

Nisbet, Robert. *Twilight of Authority*. New York: Oxford University Press, 1975.

Note. "The Outer Limits of Parental Autonomy: Withholding Medical Treatment from Children." *Ohio State Law Journal* 42 (1981), 813.

Padover, Saul K. *Jefferson*. New York: Harcourt-Brace, 1942.

Payne, George. *The Child in Human Progress*. New York: G. P. Putnam's Sons, 1916.

Pilpel, Harriet. "Minor's Rights to Medical Care." *Albany Law Review* 36 (1972), 462.

Plumb, J. H. "The Great Change in Children." *Horizon* 13 (Winter 1971), 6.

Postman, Neil. *The Disappearance of Childhood*. New York: Delacorte Press, 1982.

Radbill, Samuel. "Children in a World of Violence: A History of Child Abuse." *The Battered Child*. Chicago: University of Chicago Press, 1980.

Records of the Governor and Company of Massachusetts Bay in New England, 1642-1647.

Rheinstein, Max. *Marriage Stability, Divorce, and the Law*. Chicago: University of Chicago Press, 1972.

Rich, Spencer. "One-Parent Families Found to Increase Sharply in U.S." *Washington Post*, May 15, 1985.

Richard, John W. "Carle Zimmerman's Sociology of the Family." *The Mankind Quarterly* 22 (Fall and Winter 1982).

Richards, David A. J. "The Individual, the Family, and the Constitution: A Jurisprudential Perspective." *New York University Law Review* 55 (1980), 1.

Riga, Peter J. "The Supreme Court's View of Marriage and the Family: Tradition or Transition." *Journal of Family Law* 18 (1979-80).

Rothbard, Murray. *Education: Free and Compulsory.* Wichita, Kan.: Center for Independent Education, 1977.

Rushdoony, Rousas John. "The Trustee Family and Economics." *The Journal of Christian Reconstruction* 9 (1982-83), 204.

San Francisco Examiner, November 21, 1982.

Schaeffer, Edith. *Lifelines.* Westchester, Ill.: Crossway Books, 1982.

Schaeffer, Francis A. *A Christian Manifesto.* Westchester, Ill.: Crossway Books, 1981.

Schlafly, Phillis, editor. *Child Abuse in the Classroom.* Alton, Ill.: Pere Marquette Press, 1984; Westchester, Ill.: Crossway Books, 1984.

Schoeman, Ferdinand. "Childhood Competence and Autonomy." *Journal of Legal Studies* 12 (1983), 267.

Scott, Hilda. *Sweden's "Right to Be Human": Sex Role Equality: The Goal and the Reality.* Armonk, N.J.: M. E. Sharpe, 1982.

Shannon, William V. "Too Much, Too Soon." *New York Times,* Sept. 8, 1976.

Shearer, Lloyd. "Preventing Sexual Abuse of Children." *Parade,* May 26, 1985.

Stan, Isidore, Todd, Lewis Paul and Curtis, Merle. *Living American Documents.* New York: Harcourt, Brace and World, 1961.

Steinfels, Margaret O'Brien. *Who's Minding the Children?: The History and Politics of Day Care in America.* New York: Simon and Schuster, 1973.

Stimpson, Catherine R. *Discrimination Against Women: Congressional Hearing on Equal Rights in Education and Employment.* New York: R. R. Bowker, 1973.

Thomas, Mason P. Jr. "Child Abuse and Neglect: Historical Overview, Legal Matrix, and Social Perspectives." *North Carolina Law Review* 50 (1972), 293.

Tiffin, Susan. *In Whose Best Interest.* Westport, Conn.: Greenwood Press, 1982.

Tobak, James and Zirkel, Perry. "Home Instruction: An Analysis of the Statutes and Case Law." *University of Dayton Law Review* 8 (1982), 13.

Toffler, Alvin. *The Third Wave.* New York: Bantam Books, 1981.

Tribe, Laurence. "Childhood, Suspect Classifications, and Conclusive Presumptions: Three Linked Riddles." *Law and Contemporary Problems* 39 (1975), 8.

U. S. Constitution. Art. I and II.

Wald, Michael. "State Intervention on Behalf of 'Neglected' Children:

A Search for Realistic Standards." *Stanford Law Review* 27 (1975), 985.

Wald, Patricia. "Making Sense Out of the Rights of Youth." *Journal of the Child Welfare League of America* 55 (1975), 382.

Watson, Andrew S. "Children, Families, and Courts: Before the Best Interests of the Child and *Parham v. J. R.*" *Virginia Law Review* 66 (1980), 653.

Webster's New Collegiate Dictionary. Springfield, Mass.: G. and C. Merriam, 1975.

Weingarten, Paul. "Children's Rights: How Old Is Old Enough?" *Chicago Tribune,* February 15, 1981.

———. "Emancipation Laws: Divorce from Parents Is a Child's Legal Way Out." *Chicago Tribune,* February 16, 1981.

———. "Battle Lines Are Drawn Over a Child's Right to Sexual Privacy." *Chicago Tribune,* February 17, 1981.

———. "Rights Finally Make the Grade as the Fourth 'R' in School." *Chicago Tribune,* February 18, 1981.

Whitehead, John W. and Bird, Wendell R. *Home Education and Constitutional Liberties.* Westchester, Ill.: Crossway Books, 1984.

Whitehead, John W. *The Stealing of America.* Westchester, Ill.: Crossway Books, 1982.

Wilbur, William H. *The Making of George Washington.* Daytona Beach: Patriotic Education, Inc., 1973.

Wingo, Harvey and Freytog, Sharon N. "Decisions Within the Family: A Clash of Constitutional Rights." *Iowa Law Review* 67 (1982), 401.

Wish, Harvey. *Society and Thought in Early America.* New York: Longmans Green, 1950.

The Works of the Rev. John Witherspoon. 2d ed. Philidelphia: William Woodard, 1802.

Wu, John C. H. *Fountain of Justice.* Beaverton, Ore.: International Scholarly Book Services, 1980.

Zimmerman, Carle C. *Family and Civilization.* New York: Harper and Row, 1947.

Zimmerman, Carle C. and Cervantes, Lucious F. *Marriage and the Family.* Chicago: Henry Regnery, 1956.

INDEX

THE AUTHOR

John W. Whitehead, an attorney specializing in constitutional law, is president of the Rutherford Institute, headquartered in Manassas, Virginia. He has successfully litigated many constitutional law cases, including cases concerning the rights of parents.

Mr. Whitehead has taught constitutional law and courses on the First Amendment. He has also lectured at various law schools throughout the United States.

Mr. Whitehead has served as counsel to numerous organizations. He has also served as counsel *amicus curiae* in the United States Supreme Court and various United States Circuit Courts.

Mr. Whitehead is a member of the bars of the Supreme Courts of Virginia and Arkansas; the United States Supreme Court; the United States Courts of Appeals for the Fourth, Seventh, and Ninth Circuits; and various United States District Courts.

Mr. Whitehead has authored ten books and has coauthored others. The film version of his book *The Second American Revolution* has been made by Franky Schaeffer V Productions of Los Gatos, California. The movie has been screened in the White House and before congressional staffs in Washington, D.C. It was nationally premiered in November 1982 at the National Archives in Washington, D.C.

Mr. Whitehead has also published articles in both the *Emory Law Journal* and *Texas Tech Law Review.* Both concerned First Amendment issues.

He is married and the father of five children.

DATE DUE

ILL 3weeks			
6/25 JB			